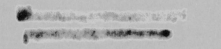

A DISTANCED LAND

The Photographs of John Pfahl

International Paper Company (formerly "The Great Falls of the Hudson"),
Corinth, New York, October 1988, from *Waterfalls,* 1988–

A DISTANCED LAND

The Photographs of John Pfahl

Essay by Estelle Jussim
Organized, with series introductions,
by Cheryl Brutvan

PUBLISHED BY
THE UNIVERSITY OF NEW MEXICO PRESS
IN ASSOCIATION WITH
ALBRIGHT-KNOX ART GALLERY

The Albright-Knox Art Gallery is supported in part by grants-in-aid from
the County of Erie and the City of Buffalo.

Library of Congress Cataloging-in-Publication Data
Pfahl, John, 1939–
    A distanced land : the photographs of John Pfahl / organized by
Cheryl Brutvan with an essay by Estelle Jussim and introductory
essays by Cheryl Brutvan.
p.   cm.
Exhibition held Nov. 16, 1990–Jan. 6, 1991 at the Albright-Knox Art Gallery.
Includes bibliographical references (p.
ISBN 0-8263-1214-4   ISBN 0-8263-1215-2 (pbk.)
1. Photography, Artistic—Exhibitions. 2. Pfahl, John, 1939–   —
Exhibitions.   I. Brutvan, Cheryl A.   II. Jussim, Estelle.
III. Albright-Knox Art Gallery.   IV. Title.
TR647.P494   1990
779'.36'092—dc20
89-70882   CIP

This book was published on the occasion of the exhibition
A Distanced Land: The Photographs of John Pfahl.

Albright-Knox Art Gallery
Buffalo, New York
November 16, 1990–January 6, 1991

The Art Institute of Chicago
Chicago, Illinois
July 27–October 6, 1991

High Museum of Art
Atlanta, Georgia
October 5, 1992–January 8, 1993

This exhibition is sponsored through the generous support of

 **MARINE MIDLAND BANK**

CONTENTS

A visit to Albright-Knox Art Gallery provides an art experience rich in diversity. Every medium is represented: painting, printmaking, drawing, sculpture, kinetic art, as well as a variety of contemporary works involving new and experimental materials. With the John Pfahl retrospective exhibition, the Gallery showcases yet another medium—photography.

Marine Midland is especially pleased and honored to sponsor the Pfahl retrospective, which celebrates and records the awesome beauty of our contemporary landscape.

Charles M. Mitschow
Regional President
Marine Midland Bank

This publication accompanies the premiere retrospective exhibition of the work of photographer John Pfahl, whose stunning and provocative images of our contemporary landscape have challenged traditional views of this familiar subject. While Pfahl has gained international recognition as the focus of numerous shows devoted to his individual series, this exhibition will be the first consideration of the artist's entire oeuvre and his influence on the field of contemporary photography. This body of work begins with the widely recognized conceptual and often humorous images from *Altered Landscapes*, and includes the majestic towers of future energy from *Power Places*, the elegant painterly views of *Arcadia Revisited*, and the recently photographed *Waterfalls* and *Smoke* series. Throughout the nine series, Pfahl has maintained professional standards of excellence and has displayed a keen sense of place and obvious delight in his subjects.

This publication would not have been possible without the diligence of curator Cheryl Brutvan, who organized the exhibition and wrote the introductions to each series of Pfahl's work. Her ability to reveal the central theme of each group enhances the illuminating commentary of the essay by Estelle Jussim. We also are grateful to Elizabeth C. Hadas, director, and Dana Asbury, editor, at the University of New Mexico Press for their enthusiastic collaboration on this project. We have enjoyed the opportunity to work together.

We offer special thanks for the generous support of Marine Midland Bank and appreciate the efforts of Charles M. Mitschow, regional president, in once again addressing the need for corporate support of the arts. I also salute Barbara Barber, development officer at the Gallery, for her work in securing this aid. We also welcome the support we have received through public funds from the New York State Council on the Arts and the National Endowment for the Arts. The Gallery also has benefited through grants-in-aid from the County of Erie and the City of Buffalo. The exhibition will travel to other venues following its premiere in Buffalo, including the Art Institute of Chicago and the High Museum of Art in Atlanta. We thank James N. Wood, director of the Art Institute of Chicago and Gudmund Vigtel, director of the High Museum of Art in Atlanta, for their willingness to offer the work of John Pfahl to audiences in other regions.

Finally, applause to John Pfahl, who has shortened the distance between viewers and the magnificent landscapes he has encountered throughout the country through his thoughtful, breathtaking imagery.

Douglas G. Schultz
Director
Albright-Knox Art Gallery

It has been a privilege to organize *A Distanced Land: The Photographs of John Pfahl*, the retrospective exhibition of the work of John Pfahl that this publication accompanies. It has also been a joy to produce this volume, which is the first to acknowledge all of the stunning series that John Pfahl has completed or that, at the time of printing, are ongoing.

We are very pleased to be co-publishing for the first time with the University of New Mexico Press. Dana Asbury, editor, is a loyal fan of the artist's work. She and designer Milenda Nan Ok Lee have been integral to the realization of this beautiful volume.

Despite an extremely hectic schedule, Estelle Jussim accepted our invitation to contribute to this project. A noted author on the subject of landscape photography, she has written a text that reveals her enduring admiration for the artist and his work.

I am especially appreciative of the skill of Mary Cochrane, the Albright-Knox Art Gallery's assistant editor of publications, who edited and coordinated this publication seemingly without difficulty. We both benefited from the advice and expertise of Karen Lee Spaulding, editor of publications. Also essential to the production of this book were Annette Masling, former librarian, and Kari Horowicz, librarian; Chris Daniels and Lucille Groth, curatorial secretaries;

Biff Henrich, photographer; Barbara Tudor, research assistant; and Margaret Noonan, intern extraordinaire in the Department of Prints and Drawings. Campos Photography Center accommodated the artist in the printing of the photographs in the exhibition, which are reproduced here.

My sincere thanks are also extended to Douglas G. Schultz, director, for his enthusiastic support of this project. I also extend my thanks to the curators of the museums participating in the tour of this exhibition: David Travis, curator, and Russ Harris, assistant to the curator, at the Art Institute of Chicago and Susan Krane, curator at the High Museum of Art in Atlanta.

Finally, it is with deep respect that I extend my thanks to John Pfahl, whose vision is inspirational, especially now as we enter the last decade of the twentieth century. The world as we know it is in increasing danger; with Pfahl's remarkable and astute responses to the landscape, transformed in his magnificent photographs, we are provoked to recognize something that could be lost forever. He has willingly participated in every aspect of this project, offering his sensitive and critical eye to even the most ordinary task. *A Distanced Land: The Photographs of John Pfahl* is a celebration of the artist's thoughtful images of a subject about which he is passionate and dedicated.

Cheryl Brutvan
Curator

For Bonnie

PLATE 1. *Moonrise over Pie Pan*, Capitol Reef National Park, Utah, October 1977

The idea becomes a machine that makes the art.
—Sol LeWitt[1]

When William Henry Fox Talbot published *The Pencil of Nature*, the first major book illustrated by mounted paper photographic prints, in the fourth decade of the nineteenth century, the idea of "Nature" was that it was the vessel, the holy text through which God revealed his glory. In fact, Nature *was* God. It was to be contemplated with reverence, with an Emersonian extravagance of adoration that still reverberates in the bravura landscape photographs of Ansel Adams.

A pity, then, that Talbot's early calotypes were unable to capture all the color and detail of Nature. With emulsions far too slow to catch wind-blown branches or stop the tumbling exuberance of rivers, insensitive to greens as well as reds, both of which were rendered as black, unable to deliver the tonalities of clouds or blue skies, landscape photography had to wait for more adequate transcriptions through wet collodion emulsions, albumen paper, and the genius of European photographers like Gustave Le Gray, Roger Fenton, and Philip Henry Delamotte in the 1850s and 1860s. The invention of faster orthochromatic film in the 1870s improved the ability of the camera to capture the details of Nature, but by that time, Nature had begun to subside into being just "nature," and ideas about what nature was and what it represented, if anything, were changing. Perhaps only in the American landscape photographs of Eadweard Muybridge and Carleton Watkins was the exaltation of Nature still celebrated, and that was because they sought out the most spectacular, the most exotic of what are now national wilderness areas. The artistic thrill of nature's most intense moments had to wait for the development and acceptance of realistic color photography in the mid-twentieth century.

Conceptions about the natural world, viewed as a series of landscapes, had been classified with considerable precision in the eighteenth century, the century which also gave us the idea of the aesthetic. Edmund Burke decided that there were specific and definable characteristics of landscapes which he noted as the *sublime*, differentiating them from the merely beautiful. Sublimity in landscape consisted of awe-inspiring, astonishing, immense silent vistas touched with terror, while beauty contained itself in round, smooth, unsurprising, more intimate, and harmonious views. Yet the term *sublime* was also used to describe Claude Lorrain's seascapes, with their effulgent skies drenched in brilliant yellows, oranges, and reds, prophetic of the explosive color that would appear in J. M. W. Turner's tempestuous canvases.

Both the Claudian sublime and Turner's incandescence have had John Pfahl's warmest admiration. A master of color landscapes himself, and one of the most original of late twentieth-century photographers, Pfahl has studied the great painters avidly. But sublimity is not his sole ambition. He has also pursued what William Gilpin and Sir Uvedale Price called the *picturesque*, a classification of landscape that requires that it be as like a painting—a picture, in other words—as possible. Gilpin and Price, two late-eighteenth-century ideologues, described in detail what elements the picturesque usually contained: twisted trees, gushing brooks, and intricately detailed flora surrounding tumbled cottage walls. These elements had to be displayed in a compositional formula that had to include a dark mass of tree announcing the foreground as it frames one edge of the picture, a middle ground usually of a body of water, and distant mountains or other rising shapes.

John Pfahl has succeeded in photographing ingenious couplings of beauty with the picturesque, as well as incorporating the sublime with both the other categories of aesthetic experience. More important, he endows his landscapes with ideas beyond the aesthetic, beyond a concern with the interpretation of nature per se or the painstaking representation of natural details so beloved by the nineteenth-century followers of John Ruskin. Pfahl is complex, a geomancer who has an almost magical touch, and a brave juggler of concepts embedded with a sumptuous and unequivocal sensuality. Each of his various projects—*Altered Landscapes, Picture Windows, Video Landscapes, Power Places, Submerged Petroglyphs, Missile/Glyphs, Arcadia Revisited*—manifests an underlying continuity that can be defined as a dedication to ideas about nature and the effects of human intervention on nature.

Ultimately this is the old dream of mankind
and of the imagination to play with
the elements of nature.
—Yves Klein and Werner Ruhnau, 1959[2]

Ideas sometimes take a long time percolating between the stimulus and the event. Thus it was with an encounter Pfahl had when he was fresh out of college and on a hitchhiking tour of Europe. It was 1961, the beginning of the decade of earthworks and pop art, conceptual art and idea art, and of a general movement that ultimately would be called postmodernism. Visiting Denmark's Nationalmuseet in Copenhagen, Pfahl entered a gallery containing a conglomeration of unfamiliar objects called *anamorphic art*. He peered into a peephole in the front of a "perspective box" the size of a large doll's house and saw what seemed to be a three-dimensional room, rather like a miniature stage set seen through a proscenium arch. Looking through another peephole at the top of the box, he discovered to his surprise that the room was a two-dimensional painted illusion created by enormously exaggerated perspective.

Pfahl, a good mathematician, was delighted and fascinated by this discovery of anamorphic illusionism. He had majored in graphic design, which after all specializes in producing effects on a two-dimensional surface (paper, usually). Over the next six or seven years he became increasingly absorbed in the problems of perception. He read voluminously, R. L. Gregory's *Eye and Brain*, E. H.

Gombrich's *Art and Illusion*, and similar books on how the eye is fooled and how visual perception can be manipulated. Saul Steinberg's *The Labyrinth*, with its visual games and unpredictable humor, became a favorite. The enigmas and paradoxes of turning two dimensions into three, and back into two, became obsessions. He began to experiment by turning the two dimensions of photographs into three by printing color pictures of trees in three-dimensional formed plastic (Fig. 1). Toward the end of the tumultuous sixties, when all media had enlarged the options of the artist, these plastic bubbles became three-dimensional wallpaper and other conceits.

In the early seventies, Pfahl, a passionate music lover, especially of opera, composed a score for percussion by making markings on trees with tape and string. This activity could be seen as the beginning of his involvement with *Altered Landscapes*. It is not hard to imagine that the anamorphic art he had encountered in Denmark, plus the years of investigating perceptual illusions, had given birth to an original idea in photography. He recognized that anamorphic representations rely upon a system of central perspective that is "not only a way of organizing a picture internally; it also offers a means of coordinating it with the position of the viewer."[3] Like most photographs, anamorphic art has a tyrannical hold on the spectator's viewpoint, a fact that permitted Pfahl to make certain manipulations like those in *Blue Right Angle, Buffalo* (Plate 4).

The seeming playfulness or even perceptual perversity of the transformations

FIGURE 1. John Pfahl, *Flowered Wallpaper*, 1974.
Photo images, butyrate plastic illustrations,
12 × 12 in. each. Courtesy of the artist.

of conventional pictorial space in *Altered Landscapes* are serious explorations of some of the oldest problems of representation. Since the Renaissance discovery of perspective, painting has involved the act of creating illusions of three dimensions on a two-dimensional surface. The more illusionistic, the more admired by the public-at-large. The object of this kind of illusionistic painting has been to tell a story, display an event, argue a moral, fictionalize history; in other words, to convey content—sometimes called "subject mat-ter"—to the eye in a way that imitates three-dimensional realities.

With the advent of photography in the first half of the nineteenth century, painting had a rival in verisimilitude if not in realistic color. As the century progressed and photography assumed more and more of the traditional func-tions of illusionistic painting, artists and art theorists sought to differentiate the two methods of visual production. By 1890—with Maurice Denis's famous comment to the effect that before it is a picture of a war horse or a nude or anything else, a painting is essentially an arrangement of colors on a flat surface—what mattered was not verisimilitude but inventiveness, decorative power, symbolism. Following a kind of inexorable logic, painting by the 1940s had become obsessively two-dimensional. Content was banished to illustra-tion, and the abstract expressionists established such a dogma of nonrepresen-tationalism that any other art was considered beneath contempt. In all this critical furor over two dimensions and three dimensions, photography, which had already been ostracized for its reliance on content, continued to be banished from museums to the realm of photojournalism and popular culture.

Photography, however, made a strong recovery in the sixties, when concep-tual artists, especially those involved in earthworks or landworks, discovered that the way to make their wilderness and desert efforts available to the general public was precisely through the kind of documentation available with pho-tography. "Ironically, the documents often assumed a somewhat disconcerting

FIGURE 2. Robert Smithson, aerial view of
Spiral Jetty, 1970.
Black rock, salt crystals, earth, red water (algae).
Coil, 1,500 × c. 15 ft.
Estate of Robert Smithson;
courtesy of John Weber Gallery, New York.
Photograph by Gianfranco Gorgoni, New York.

fine art, pictorial quality, especially when presented in a conventional gallery setting."[4] The landscape documents of striking works like Robert Smithson's *Spiral Jetty*, 1970 (Fig. 2), were considered not only records of monumental earthworks, but also photographs of considerable beauty. Other conceptual or idea artists, such as Ed Ruscha, relied upon photography as documentation as well, but cared little if the pictures were admirable in themselves. The point is that photographs began to appear in museums and galleries as art works or parts of art works. Thus the visual, sensual world was restored to a public generally irritated by museum displays consisting of nothing but sheets of typing paper on which appeared arcane verbal "ideas."

Given the various contexts of the sixties and the early seventies, John Pfahl happened to make his own entrance into the art world at precisely the right time. *Altered Landscapes*, a photographic record of "fine art, pictorial quality," was simultaneously a unique contribution to landscape, to color photography, and to idea art. It immediately established his reputation. The significant difference between Pfahl's interventions in three-dimensional reality and permanent installations like Smithson's is that Pfahl left no trace of his handiwork after the photograph was taken. To defy perspective, for example, Pfahl meticulously attached pieces of tape to columns, fooling the spectator into believing that they are geometric marks on the surface of the photograph because they seem to be all the same size. This seemingly simple exercise took hours of mathematical analysis, marking out the desired anamorphosis on the glass of his view camera, reviewing with Polaroid shots to check the correctness of his illusions, waiting for the right light, making the exposure, and finally removing all traces of his intervention into three-dimensional reality. He followed the same procedures with the landscape *Moonrise over Pie Pan*, 1977 (Plate 1).

Pfahl remarks about *Moonrise* that it took "a very hectic hour [to set up] as

I could not know exactly where on the horizon the moon would appear, or how large it would be in relation to the pie pan. I kept making minor adjustments of vantage point, camera direction, and pie pan proximity, and was extremely lucky to make an exposure when everything was in the right balance."[5] It should be noted that this parody of Ansel Adams's famous *Moonrise over Hernandez* was produced in the spirit of admiration, not mockery; it represents Pfahl's delight in complex perceptual exercises.

Because it has been remarked that *Altered Landscapes* has an affiliation with conceptual or idea art—that is, rather than with simple illusionistic representationalism—Pfahl observes, "Although I have never been a Conceptual artist with a capital *C*, there has always been a conceptual bias to my work."[6] Unlike many conceptual artists of the sixties, however, Pfahl "was never interested in the elimination of the materiality of the art object in favor of pure 'message' and, while much of my work is thought out ahead of time, I do not unswervingly adhere to a preconceived formula."[7] After he was well into his series of altered landscapes, he saw several works by Jan Dibbets, a Dutch conceptualist who used photography to embody his perspective corrections. Pfahl immediately realized that his photographs were quite different. "Instead of presenting the dry bones of an idea in the most direct way possible, I was more interested in fleshing out the skeleton with color, atmosphere, context and extra-photographic references. I was after a certain richness of experience."[8] While he admired the work of John Baldessari, the California artist whose playful Duchampian paradoxes were the quintessence of the photographically recorded conceptual performance, Pfahl had no interest in Baldessari's preoccupation with words, so typical of conceptual art in general. That Pfahl preferred visual magnificence to unadorned concept became obvious in his next project, *Picture Windows*.

To my mother, who introduced me, at an early age,
to photography and to the concept of
a really clean window.
—John Pfahl, Dedication, *Picture Windows*

The illusionism mentioned earlier in connection with the development of perspective was also at least partially the outcome of optical and mathematical discoveries during the Renaissance. Window glass was becoming popular and cheap enough for the bourgeoisie to enjoy. The so-called Renaissance window effect is precisely that: a painting was like an open window through which the viewer gazed at scenes carefully organized within the rectangle of the window frame. Landscape especially was to be seen as if through a large window. Having studied art history and now increasingly interested in specific painters, among them Caspar David Friedrich, Arnold Böcklin, Hokusai, George Inness, and

Charles Burchfield, Pfahl embarked on a new series. *Picture Windows* can be considered as a commentary on the entire concept of the Renaissance window as well as on landscape photography in general. He came to this project in 1978, when what was then regarded as "large-scale" color photography, with prints averaging 16 × 20 inches, was becoming an influential visual environment. Now, of course, color prints are much larger. Pfahl had done his own darkroom work for *Altered Landscapes*, with spectacular results. He has continued this arduous practice throughout his career.

A new influence had entered his conceptual base. This was the aleatory approach of John Cage, an unconventional conceptualist composer who equated audience noise with formal music itself, and who once let a multitude of radios blare onstage in lieu of traditional instrumentation. Cage, like Merce Cunningham, regularly consulted *I Ching* and followed its chance directives. Pfahl was ready to accept chance as an element in his pictures. In *Picture Windows*, Pfahl permitted stains, condensation, spots of dirt, and other marks to remain on the glass windows and meticulously recorded these along with the view beyond. His camera work here was ingenious: "He set the focus so that everything from inside the window-sill to infinity would be resolved into a consistently sharp image, compressing all into a shallow 'in-focus sandwich.'"[9] What this produced was an image radically different from how human perception usually registers a scene. Printing extensive black borders around the windows emphasized the brilliance of the landscape or urbanscape outside.

Pfahl included in *Picture Windows* the hypercolor image called *Garden of the Gods Loop Drive, Colorado Springs, Colorado* [see Plate 29], so much like a picture postcard that the startling topography of the scene looks unusually bizarre. But this landscape view has reverberations in the history of photography, in all the government expeditionary records made by Timothy O'Sullivan, William Henry Jackson, A. J. Russell, among many others who journeyed west to find novel sites. In *228 Grant Avenue, San Francisco, California* (Plate 26), Pfahl gives us a picture window that opens onto a view of appallingly close brick walls containing a window filled in with cinder blocks. (What compulsive contractor perpetrated such a monstrosity?) Another image, *10 South Park Avenue, Buffalo, New York*, makes exquisite abstract patterns out of the wire-caged and broken-glass windows of a warehouse. Can we fail to recognize that not everyone in America is permitted to enjoy a view of a pristine landscape? Do those of us who can afford to buy the book *Picture Windows* know how rare is the family that can build a house, say, facing the sun-smitten cliffs in Springdale, Utah? Implicit comment—the unspoken concept—resides in almost every image.

Before he began his controversial series called *Power Places*, Pfahl spent the winter months of 1981, when snow and cold prevented his working outdoors in Buffalo, making what he describes as *Video Landscapes* (Plates 31–41). These indoor photographs, in grainy black-and-white television textures, are reminiscent of American pictorialist landscapes from around the turn of the century.

Poetic, lyrical, crepuscular, with many of the photographs intending to reveal what Paul Caponigro calls "the landscape beyond the landscape,"[10] pictorialism was largely a venture into symbolism. Pfahl's video landscapes are astonishing revelations of what the still photograph can make of the moving electronic image.

Et in Arcadia Ego
(I—Death—am also in Arcadia).[11]

If *Altered Landscapes* relied dramatically upon surprise, visual wit, paradox, and parody, and *Picture Windows* relied upon the Renaissance window—literally—as well as on the theatrical effects of looking at a stage through a proscenium arch, then Pfahl's next project, *Power Places*, at first glance seemed to be straightforward landscape photography, with no hidden analogies or messages. Oh, there were surprises enough: Pfahl's photograph of the monumental Hoover Dam, for example, reveals that the shadow cast by the dam's own turrets resembles the shadow of a monstrous air force superbomber (Plate 60).

In *Power Places*, John Pfahl presents some of his most paradoxical ideas, ideas that seem to pose questions rather than offer answers. Since the early nineteenth century and the intrusion of the railroad and heavy industry into the then unspoiled wilderness, Americans have pondered the crucial issues surrounding technology and the environment. Pfahl provides no exaggerated condemnation of nuclear plants or other energy-producing technologies, despite his knowledge of their potential danger. To consider his pictures of power places as being ironic, rather than complimentary or condemnatory, probably requires both sophistication and a proenvironmental, antinuclear attitude. It is unfortunately just as easy to decide that these stunning landscapes depict the successful—and peaceful—marriage of power and beauty, an opinion that the nuclear industry naturally encourages. Pfahl has discovered that pronuclear groups believe he is on their side, while antinuclear groups think he is on theirs. He acknowledges that he attempted to keep *Power Places* as neutral as possible. "I'm not interested in pushing simple opinions or making propagandistic statements. It seems to me that when more than one message is presented in a work of art, a tension is created that cries out for resolution."[12] People who are conditioned by advertising photography and most photojournalism "expect an unambiguous message and find my work perplexing. However, I would hope that most viewers are provoked by the deliberately fostered tension to think more deeply about the complexity of the issues."[13] The intention is to make people relate to the implications of an image.

The concept behind the pictures, at least one of which uses Turneresque color (see *Rancho Seco Nuclear Plant, Sacramento, California*, Plate 62) is obviously the coupling of beauty with implicit or potential terror. Not a new idea in art, although his treatment of the subject is certainly different. (It evokes the first line of Rainer Maria Rilke's poem, "For beauty is only the beginning of terror...") A beauty/terror image that also comes instantly to mind is Eugène Delacroix's *Death of Sardanapalus,* in which a dying tyrant has his harem wives slaughtered beside his enormous bed. It is as sensual as can be imagined, yet frightful at the same time. What brought to mind the unlikely connection between the Delacroix painting of erotic horror and Pfahl's *Power Places* is something Pfahl once observed about his landscapes: they are erotic. There is something sexual, he admits, about traversing (often on foot) huge tracts of land in order to possess parts of them in photographs. In the case of *Power Places,* the eroticism is largely expressed through color; the terror is implicit in the content.

Power Places not only presented more and more complex ideas that willy-nilly engaged political as well as emotional responses, but it also marked the beginning of Pfahl's fascination with luminist paintings and photographs. After an interval that saw him invited to join a group recording petroglyphs in the Southwest, he combined pictures of petroglyphs with ominous images of missiles at Albuquerque's National Atomic Museum. Pfahl then embarked on a project that involved new and even more splendid landscape photography. The portent was undoubtedly the miraculously beautiful *Four Corners Power Plant,* Farmington, New Mexico (Plates 50–51), with its striking division of spaces and balance of light to dark.

We want the Exact and the Vast;
we want our Dreams,
and our Mathematics.
—Ralph Waldo Emerson[14]

Many of the aesthetic issues in landscape imagery come to a sharp focus in Pfahl's photographs of Niagara. The Niagara project, entitled *Arcadia Revisited: Niagara River and Falls from Lake Erie to Lake Ontario*, is a pivotal work for anyone studying John Pfahl's approaches to landscape.

Possessing a profound interest in nineteenth-century pictorial conventions, now living in Buffalo not far from the world-famous Niagara Falls, and having achieved a notable national and international reputation, Pfahl was the obvious choice for a commission to photograph the river and falls from the point of view of a late-nineteenth-century graphic artist, the etcher Amos W. Sangster. In making his proposal to the committee, Pfahl promised "to spend my days hiking along the river, exploring with passion its nooks and crannies."[15] He would find the places where Sangster stood and use his etchings as the appropriate point of departure, noting what was new and what had remained since the publication of Sangster's Niagara etchings in 1886.

As could be expected, Pfahl delivered magnificent color photographs, keeping to his proposals vis-à-vis Sangster. These images more than adequately demonstrated Pfahl's observation about Niagara, to the effect that "the nineteenth century is palpably evident under the veneer of present-day reality."[16] To his surprise, he found that the "river I had seen in the old prints and paintings was still very much in place. To be sure, an accretion of bridges, hydroelectric installations, and chemical plants had been added to the scene, but similar intrusions had already been present in the mid-1800s."[17] Intensively studying the artistic conventions and ideologies that had prevailed in Sangster's time, Pfahl recognized that the predominant aesthetic approach even in the 1880s was that of the picturesque. He also realized that what the late-nineteenth-century bourgeoisie desired in a landscape was a formula described by Kenneth Clark: "A peaceful scene, with water in the foreground reflecting a luminous sky and set off by dark trees."[18] It was a formula out of Claude Lorrain's light-struck landscapes via the Barbizon painters. It was also dependent on luminist strategies with color and composition. A perfect embodiment of this formula is Pfahl's amazingly accurate evocation in *Two Miles Below the Falls* (Plate 88), which combines elements of luministic and picturesque aesthetics.

The favored aesthetic of painters like Fitz Hugh Lane, John Kensett, Sanford Gifford, and even at times Frederic Edwin Church and Albert Bierstadt, luminism moved away from depicting the sublime as defined by Edmund Burke, with its terrors and vertiginous depths, toward "the feeling of spiritual calm man derived from the contemplation of boundless panoramas and light-filled landscapes that emphasized the illusion of space, infinity, and quiet."[19] The emphasis was entirely on atmospheric tonalism, and stressed an impersonal touch that seemed in direct contradiction to the equal emphasis on intimacy that prevailed between the artist and nature. Light was the leading actor, pure brilliant light.

Robert Adams, an eminent American landscape photographer, has remarked that "all landscapes are defined by the sun,"[20] and he insists that what is of primary importance in an image is the animating part played by light. Luminism was not, however, only pure light but included compositional devices that the art historian Barbara Novak calls "luminist classicism."[21] This classicism, which harks back to Poussin's painterly strategies, reveals itself in the mathematical and geometric correlations that create planes stepping back rhythmically, parallel to the picture plane, with occasional vertical and diagonal accents. "Structure, form, tone, light are all subject to the subtlest discretions of calculated control. These minute and economic discriminations release poetic rather than cerebral effects."[22] In another statement, Novak observes that luminism is conceptual. Overall, of course, luminism reflected the intense passion for nature that was the equivalent of religious fervor in mid-nineteenth-century America.

When John Pfahl was a boy, his parents took him for frequent hikes in wilderness areas. Recent immigrants from Germany, they were filled with enthusiasm for nature and even persuaded the boy that "Nature is our church!"[23] They gave Pfahl a lasting interest in transcendentalism, which German philosophers had grafted onto American ideologies during the early nineteenth century. Nature has been a consuming passion with Pfahl, and his vision of it has been on the grand scale.

Photographers worshipped nature long before Ansel Adams hyped the wilderness. William Henry Jackson found both the picturesque and the sublime in western landscapes, and, as Barbara Novak suggests, western photographers also produced luminist images. Luminism in photography included "the use of crystalline light, love of atmospheric phenomena, an appreciation for the transcendent spiritual beauty of nature, love of flat, open, very palpable space."[24] Timothy O'Sullivan managed to capture a true luminist moment in his *Summits of the Uinta Mountains*, 1868–69 (Fig. 3), where an absolutely still lake perfectly reflects a fringe of ponderosas and a placid mountain. There were many accidentally luminist pictures: with the slow emulsions that could not capture the rapid motion of rivers or wind across ponds, still mirror-like lakes were the ideal setting for luminist attempts.

Among several pictures in Pfahl's *Arcadia Revisited* that fit the luminist bill are *Summer Sun over Strawberry Island* and *Fort Niagara from Niagara-on-the-Lake* (Plate 90). The setting sun in the Strawberry Island view glistens on an expanse of flat, open space; the atmosphere has achieved a transcendent tonality of color, while the silhouetted island intersects the total area as if it were a stepping stone into infinity. Fort Niagara once again offers brilliant light reflecting on a broad expanse of water, with the dark silhouette floating on just the right division of space.

FIGURE 3. Timothy O'Sullivan, *Summits of the Uinta Mountains*, 1868–69. Black-and-white photograph, 4³/₄ × 6³/₄ in. Courtesy National Archives, Washington, D.C.

As regards luminism in general, Weston Naef believes that "photography perhaps even surpasses painting in realizing some effects, such as rendering the immediacy of the observed phenomena."[25] Photography demanding "the most direct possible expression of the artists' intense concentration on nature [the picture became] an embodiment of pure thought."[26] Some of Pfahl's pictures in *Arcadia Revisited* have none of the calm of luminism, but are such intense concentrations on specific moments of the rampaging Niagara River that they seem to connect directly with the viewers' thought processes.

Seneca Ray Stoddard, Louise Deshong Woodbridge, and Henry L. Rand were among the many landscape photographers of the 1890s and early 1900s who pursued the landscape aesthetic, making luminous skies and still waters the centers of their compositions. Occasionally, luminist approaches were adopted by some of the photographers who joined the pictorialist Photo-Secession under Alfred Stieglitz, but these were relatively few. Even the later f/64 group—among them Edward Weston, Paul Strand, and Imogen Cunningham—whose sharp focus might lead you to expect their appreciation of the precise luminists, did not produce any substantially luminist oeuvre. Perhaps it is not until Pfahl and landscape photographers like Richard Misrach and Joel Meyerowitz that anything resembling luminism reappeared. It is important to recognize that color photography suited to luminist effects was not possible until the 1940s. Even with the widespread acceptance of color in the 1970s and 1980s, there are still many landscape photographers who prefer black and white. Outstanding among these is Robert Adams, who fascinates with his urban, desert, and mountain pictures, but who rarely—albeit impressively—photographs still waters (see *From the Missouri West* for several striking examples). Since Adams insists on including signs of human passage, the silence demanded by luminism is instead filled with the memory of screeching motorbikes and sandrovers.

Arcadia Revisited established John Pfahl once again as an original. There are few color photographers who can match the intensity of his vision and the beauty of his results. Eliot Porter certainly captures the stunning detail, the gorgeous ravine, the palpitating blossom, but his is not the panoramic and theatrical splendor of Pfahl's best works. One talented color photographer who has been cited as having a conceptual approach somewhat similar to Pfahl's is Joel Sternfeld, who gives us a view of the world "in which provocative questions must suffice."[27] Joel Meyerowitz, acclaimed as a supreme color artist, makes sumptuous statements about sky, beach, and sea in his *Cape Light* series. However, he does not seek the tensions Pfahl presented in, say, *Power Places*. Few artists have been able to evoke the glories of grand master landscape paintings, and at the same time embed the hint of provocative questions in images as well as John Pfahl.

All art (after Duchamp) is conceptual (in nature)
because art only exists conceptually.
—Joseph Kosuth[28]

Occasionally, attempts are made to separate Pfahl's total oeuvre into two distinct subdivisions: the conceptual on the one hand, as in *Altered Land-scapes, Picture Windows, Power Places, Video Landscapes, Submerged Petro-glyphs, Missile/Glyphs,* and luminist on the other, as in some of *Power Places* and much of *Arcadia Revisited*. I would suggest that luminism is also conceptual, since it demands strict adherence to a set of principles of picture-making and it stresses certain aspects of light. These are ideas, after all. Pfahl's style is an idea. So is his content. In the broadest sense, John Pfahl is a conceptual artist to whom the "idea" is a tension between the observable and the implicit. Without in any way being a propagandist or even a polemicist, Pfahl's pictures imply a high regard for nature and a respect for the environment. As I once noted in another context, it is almost impossible for a single photograph to state both the problem *and* the solution.[29] Pfahl contents himself with stating the problem, hoping that his viewers will look beyond the beautiful surfaces, the astonishingly perfect paradoxes.

Ansel Adams's bravura pictures, especially his many operatic and melodramatic shots of Yosemite Valley, ask that we disengage ourselves from the world of human presence in order to recreate for ourselves an unsullied view of the world. Pfahl chooses differently. In *Picture Windows*, the world was sullied by whatever stained the windows. In *Power Places*, the viewer had to acknowledge that nuclear power plants could sully the world permanently. Pfahl's series of drowned, invisible petroglyphs (see Plates 63–71) indicate that we can deliberately destroy our own history. His *Missile/Glyphs* (see Plates 72–81), which combine petroglyphs with atomic weapons, again prophesied the imminent danger to any view of any world. His current projects, like *Smoke*, carry the implications of these hazards further, as even in the midst of a gorgeous abstraction of smoke and sky the viewer remembers that chemical pollution from industrial plants poses an unremitting, ongoing health threat that cannot, should not be ignored. Pfahl does not ask the viewer to indulge in mere passive contemplation, even though it must be admitted that the unbridled beauty of his landscapes is a temptation. Pfahl asks that we think. We shall have to wait for the completion of the new projects, *Waterfalls* and *Smoke*, to see what he will ask us to think about these new ideas.

In reviewing his own career, and responding to questions concerning the fact that many of today's photographers are now drawing and painting directly on photographic prints, Pfahl wrote a long response which deserves attention here:

> First, I believe that photographers can do whatever they please with their photographs—scratch, stitch, draw, or paint. Some of my favorite artists work in this manner.
>
> At the moment, it does not seem applicable to my work or ideas. I dealt with a number of those possibilities in the sixties, when many other photographers were also stretching the boundaries of the medium. . . .
>
> When I turned to *Altered Landscapes* I kept playing around with that attitude—but I placed my handwork into the scene instead of on the

surface of the print. . . . The pictures, however, on a very basic level, had to do with my personal "touch."

After that series of pictures, it became less important for me to become so intimately involved. As I moved back from the subject in *Picture Windows* and then in *Power Places* my own hand was replaced with the intimation of a more dominant and impersonal hand on the scene: the pressure of humankind on the lay of the land.

. . . I like the possibility of an illusion of seamless reality. I am in love with the way things look and the way that light flows over a scene picking out meaning from the jumble of reality. I am in love with the syntax of the large format color negative and print and how beautifully it can re-represent the complexities organized by that flow of light.[10]

For his love of his medium, and his love of the world, John Pfahl can indeed be called a passionate observer.

1. Quoted in Joseph Kosuth, "Art after Philosophy," in Gregory Battcock, *Idea Art* (New York: Dutton, 1973), p. 74.

2. Quoted in Carla Gottlieb, *Beyond Modern Art* (New York: Dutton, 1976), p. 302.

3. Fred Leeman, *Hidden Images: Games of Perception, Anamorphic Art, Illusion from the Renaissance to the Present* (New York: Abrams, 1976), p. 47.

4. H. H. Arnason, *History of Modern Art: Painting, Sculpture, Architecture, Photography*, 3rd ed. Revised and updated by Daniel Wheeler (New York: Abrams, 1986), p. 575.

5. Correspondence from John Pfahl, September 9, 1989.

6. Ibid.

7. Ibid.

8. Ibid.

9. Edward Bryant, Introduction to *Picture Windows: Photographs by John Pfahl* (Boston: New York Graphic Society, 1987), p. 3.

10. Kenneth Clark, quoted in Estelle Jussim and Elizabeth Lindquist-Cock, *Landscape as Photograph* (New Haven: Yale University Press, 1985), p. 65.

11. See Sally Eauclaire's discussion in *New Color/New Work* (New York: Abbeville, 1984), p. 182.

12. Correspondence from Pfahl, September 9, 1989.

13. Ibid.

14. Quoted in Barbara Novak, *American Painting in the Nineteenth Century* (New York: Praeger, 1969), p. 120.

15. John Pfahl, quoted in Sandra H. Olsen, Foreword to *Arcadia Revisited: Niagara River and Falls from Lake Erie to Lake Ontario* (Albuquerque: University of New Mexico Press, 1988), p. 13.

16. Quoted in Estelle Jussim, "Arcadian Vistas: John Pfahl's Niagara," in *Arcadia Revisited*, p. 26.

17. John Pfahl, "Artist's Statement," in *Arcadia Revisited*, p. 53.

18. Kenneth Clark, quoted in Jussim, "Arcadian Vistas," in *Arcadia Revisited*, p. 26.

19. Earl A. Powell, "Luminism and the American Sublime," in John Wilmerding, ed.,

American Light: The Luminist Movement 1850–1875 (New York: Harper & Row for the National Gallery of Art, 1980), p. 69.

20. Robert Adams, Introduction to Daniel Wolf, ed. *The American Space: Meaning in Nineteenth-Century Landscape Photography* (Middletown, Conn.: Wesleyan University Press, 1983), p. 3.

21. Barbara Novak, "On Defining Luminism," in *American Light*, p. 23.

22. Ibid.

23. Conversations with John Pfahl, June 1987.

24. Weston Naef, "New Eyes—Luminism in Photography," in *American Light*, p. 288.

25. Ibid.

26. Ibid.

27. Sally Eauclaire, *New Color/New Work*, p. 242.

28. Joseph Kosuth, "Art after Philosophy," in *Idea Art*, p. 80.

29. See Estelle Jussim, "Propaganda and Persuasion," in *Observations: Essays on Documentary* (Carmel, California: Friends of Photography, 1984), *Untitled* series 35.

30. Correspondence from Pfahl, September 9, 1989.

John Pfahl had already explored and extended the traditional boundaries of the art object when he began his series of *Altered Landscapes* in 1974. While colleagues deftly manipulated the surfaces of photographs in various ways in the early seventies—through drawing and collage, for example—Pfahl remained uninterested in such additions (he was admittedly "unable to draw"). Rather, he completed a series of sculptural photographs—shaped plastic reliefs upon which he had screenprinted photographic images of details from the natural world.

Rarely is inspiration attributed to a singular historical event, and in the milieu of this period, *Altered Landscapes* evolved not only from Pfahl's continued consideration of the unique qualities of photography, but also, as has been the case with each succeeding series of work, from his responses to visual stimuli. The very first altered landscape, however, was the result of a collaborative project with composer and musician David Gibson. Pfahl has noted that "some of my earliest memories are of listening to music," and the idea of producing a photographic and musical score appealed to him. Although a translation of the "score" from photograph to performance was unrealized, the process of altering the landscape—in this case by putting colored tape on trees—held unlimited possibilities for Pfahl. By adding to a landscape temporary mark-making devices such as string, tape, rope, foil, balls, even food, Pfahl fabricated an illusion that denied the reality of depth and perspective in the photographic image and appeared to be instead a manipulation of the surface of his print.

Pfahl's alterations were frequently elaborate and always meticulously executed, yet his deep reverence of nature prohibited him from molesting any natural setting. Pfahl would sketch the desired composition of an illusion on a black-and-white Polaroid of the scene or on clear plastic overlaying the groundglass of his view camera.

That each image within this extensive series is strikingly successful is testimony to Pfahl's thoughtful approach and astute sense of observation. The artist found suitable and challenging landscapes from coast to coast and on the islands of Hawaii and Bermuda. The seemingly perfect illusions composed in each landscape, frequently laden with humor, were inspired by elements both obviously a part of, as well as obviously missing from, a scene. Occasionally, information peculiarly relevant to a location served as a resource, as in the case of *Triangle*, 1975 (Plate 11). The humor so evident in many of these images is gentle fun, sometimes poked at monuments in the history of landscape photography.

The 131 images that make up *Altered Landscapes* brought wide acclaim to their creator not only for the brilliance of his idea, but also for his willingness to address a subject—the landscape—that was easily trivialized in the medium of photography. This series revealed, above all else, Pfahl's great technical facility and his continuing love of both photography and the landscape.

C.B.

PLATE 2. *Music I*, Ellicottville, New York, May 1974

PLATE 3. *Pink Rock Rectangle*, Artpark, Lewiston, New York, August 1975

PLATE 4. *Blue Right-angle*, Albright-Knox Art Gallery, Buffalo, New York,
September 1975

PLATE 5. *Double Diamond*, Penland, North Carolina, June 1975

PLATE 6. *Red Setters in Red Field*, Charlotte, North Carolina, April 1976

PLATE 7. *Red Arrow*, Roan Mountain, North Carolina, June 1975

PLATE 8. *Shed with Blue Dotted Lines*, Penland, North Carolina, June 1975

PLATE 9. *Marsh Grass and Hammock*, Pine Island, Florida, February 1977

PLATE 10. *Australian Pines*, Fort DeSoto, Florida, February 1977

PLATE 11. *Triangle*, Bermuda, August 1975

PLATE 12. *Net and Ship,* "The Sophia," Boston, Massachusetts, June 1978

PLATE 13. *Wave, Lave, Lace*, Pescadero Beach, California, March 1978

PLATE 14. *Canyon Point*, Zion National Park, Utah, October 1977

PLATE 15. *Rock Opening*, Big Sur, California, December 1980

PLATE 16. *Moose and Arrow*, Grand Teton National Park, Wyoming, September 1977

PLATE 17. *The Grand Teton with Dotted Line*, Grand Teton National Park,
Wyoming, August 1977

PLATE 18. *Geological Demarcations*, Garden of the Gods, Colorado Springs,
Colorado, August 1977

PLATE 19. *Slanting Orange Lines*, Hell's Half Acre, Wyoming, September 1977

PLATE 20. *Great Salt Lake Angles*, Great Salt Lake, Utah, October 1977

The elaborate sets constructed before photographing an altered landscape usually require lengthy preparations and always the cooperation of the weather.
Pfahl's desire to spend less time fabricating a composition, as well as his wish
to extend his photography season into the winter months, contributed to his
idea to photograph landscapes from indoors. *Picture Windows* was also, however, the next logical step in the artist's inquiry into perception and illusion.
Experimentation with larger format prints was also occurring at this time, and
Pfahl rose to the challenge offered by the 16-×-20-inch print that is considered
ordinary today.

The significance of the window and the view found within its frame has
been discussed often in the history of art. The experience of gazing through a
window is parallel to that of the photographer who peers through his view-
finder at a chosen image. Although each window Pfahl selected held the potential of being shot in dozens of variations—made possible by the use of several
lenses of different focal lengths, ranging from wide-angle to telephoto, and by
various placements of his view camera about the room—his primary goal was
to achieve the illusion that there was, in fact, only one possible view. He
accomplished this through a calculated manipulation of the focus that erased
the depth of the scene. All elements within view—whether in the foreground

or receding far into space—were now equally focused within the picture plane. Pfahl rarely left obstructions within the borders of the windowpanes, removing draperies and shades and leaving only those interior objects that served as a formal element in the composition or that he responded to intuitively. The extended black border recreates the sensation of the picture window looming before the photographer; the larger format of the print contributes to this illusion as well.

The early images in the series were familiar, rather than picturesque, views, including *Pingry Hill Road*, 1979 (Plate 25), and *Rochester, New York*, 1979, a wintry landscape seen through an undistinguished pane of glass on the campus of Rochester Institute of Technology. Others were spectacular, found during travels devoted to the search for suitable views. Pfahl found many views in the homes and offices of strangers, who graciously allowed him to enter once his intentions were understood. Owners were usually thrilled to have a focal point of their environment immortalized, and delighted in sharing something precious with an anonymous public.

The significance of the contrast between the brick wall found in the view in *228 Grant Avenue, San Francisco, California*, 1980 (Plate 26), and the spectacle of the mountain in *One Alpenrose Drive, Ketchum, Idaho*, 1980 (Plate 28), cannot be underestimated. Pfahl did not intend a sociological comment on the fact that some cannot choose their view while others are able to acquire it, yet it is often an integral part of the interpretation of this series. This discussion is a tribute to the artist's ability to create an image layered with meaning. Of equal significance to the reading of these images is a realization that Pfahl had while in the midst of photographing this series, that even the wildest and most remote landscape is contained within someone's picture window.

C.B.

PLATE 21. *11000 SW 57th Avenue, Miami, Florida,* March 1979

PLATE 22. *1901 NW 55th Terrace, Gainesville, Florida,* March 1979

PLATE 23. *1390 South Dixie Highway, Coral Gables, Florida,* March 1979

PLATE 24. *797 Potomac Avenue, Buffalo, New York*, September 1981

PLATE 25. *Pingry Hill Road, Andover, New York*, October 1979

PLATE 26. *228 Grant Avenue, San Francisco, California,* December 1980

PLATE 27. *Boots Brown Drive, Gimlet, Idaho*, March 1980

PLATE 28. *One Alpenrose Drive, Ketchum, Idaho,* April 1980

PLATE 29. *Garden of the Gods Loop Drive, Colorado Springs, Colorado,* July 1980

PLATE 30. *Kaanapali Coast, Maui, Hawaii,* March 1978

Pfahl lived in Rochester, New York, from 1968 to 1972, a community full of opportunities in photography. The International Museum of Photography at George Eastman House offered Pfahl exposure to the landmark images in the history of photography and the masters who created them, a subject he had embraced in graduate school. The innovative programming of the Visual Studies Workshop also presented exceptional learning opportunities, including visits by eminent scholars. In 1981, Pfahl participated in a workshop, taught by Tom Shillea, devoted to the platinum/palladium printing process. More commonly associated with turn-of-the-century techniques, the process particularly interested Pfahl because the final result demands intimate contact between the artist and the materials. The result is an entirely handcrafted product quite unlike contemporary color printing, in which a large part of the process is automatic.

Even more appealing to Pfahl was the recognition that in this process, the image actually becomes part of the paper support rather than lying on the paper surface, as in most photographic processes: the emulsion sinks into the fibers of the paper so that image and support are permanently united. This concept took on even greater significance at this time, when discussions regarding the impermanence of color photographs abounded.

Continuing to work indoors, Pfahl acquired a black-and-white monitor from which he photographed landscapes found in daily television programming. The idea was a logical step in the artist's observations of found landscapes, removing him even further physically from his subject; it also became a contemporary extension of the window in art. The final print, as a result of the platinum/palladium process, was richly toned and heavily textured, and recalled images from earlier eras, such as those of the photo-pictorialists. These historical works were an integral part of Pfahl's vocabulary; his compositions harken back to those of Coburn and Steichen, but their titles reveal their contemporary and popular sources.

C.B.

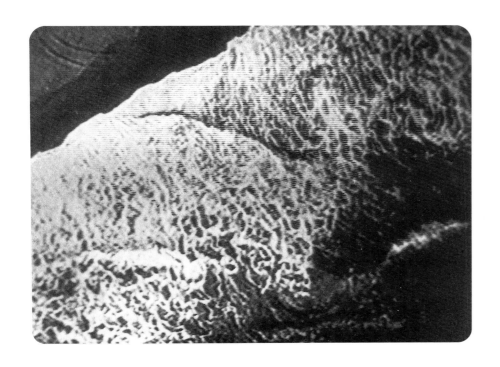

PFV-1-A / KNOT'S LANDING / CBS-TV

PLATE 31.

PFV-2-A / FANTASY ISLAND / ABC-TV

PLATE 32.

PFV-3-A / MASTERPIECE THEATER: SUNSET SONG / PBS-TV

PFV-7-A / MASTERPIECE THEATER: THERESE RAQUIN / PBS-TV

PLATE 33.

PLATE 34.

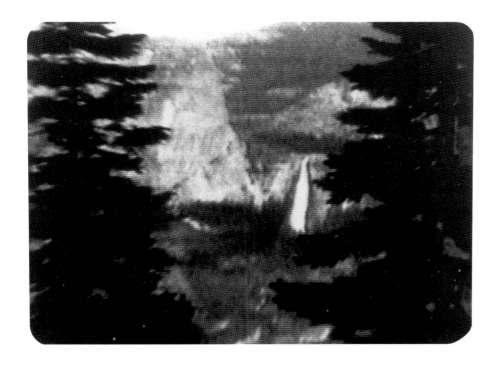

PFV-12-B / SHOCK OF THE NEW: THE VIEW FROM THE EDGE / PBS-TV

PLATE 35.

PFV-15-D / AMERICAN ODYSSEY / PBS-TV

PLATE 36.

PFV-4-A / MASTERCARD TRAVELER CHEQUES/ CBS-TV

PFV-14-D / SUNDAY MORNING: STORM OVER PARADISE / CBS-TV

PLATE 37.

PLATE 38.

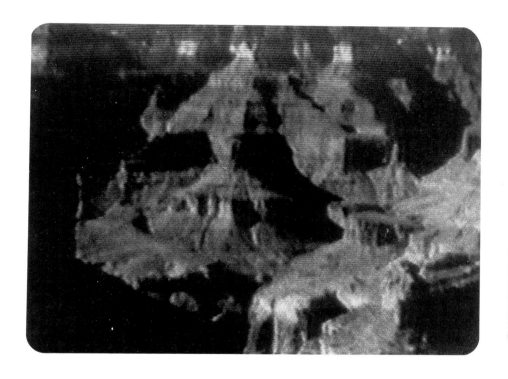

PFV-13-A / NATIONAL PARKS: PLAYGROUND OR PARADISE / PBS-TV

PLATE 39.

PFV-9-A / ETOSHA: PLACE OF DRY WATER / PBS-TV

PLATE 40.

PFV-15-A / AMERICAN ODYSSEY / PBS-TV

PLATE 41.

The stunning sight of an oil refinery surrounded by a glorious landscape bathed
in the brilliant light of the Southwest provoked John Pfahl to consider a subject
he had been acutely aware of, but had avoided: the inherent conflict between
nature and industry. Since the advent of the Industrial Revolution, the need
to satisfy civilization's ever-increasing demand for power has produced a tense
relationship between the manufactured and the natural world, one that often
verges on disaster, and at times, realizes destruction. One need only cite the
accidents at the Three Mile Island and Chernobyl nuclear energy plants, or
the more recent oil spill in Prince William Sound, to call up horrific images
of grand proportions. It was with the series *Power Places* that Pfahl first
addressed this complex subject, whose ramifications pervade all of our lives.

San Onofre Nuclear Generating Station, *San Clemente, California*, June,
1981 (Plate 59), the first image in the series, encouraged Pfahl to continue
seeking out nuclear generating plants as his primary subject. The plants are
monumental structures, typically situated in areas of incomparable beauty.
The consistent identification of these generating stations with traditional names
of the area, such as Crystal River and Peach Bottom, appeared tied to the ideals
of nineteenth-century romanticism. The concept of harnessing nature has been
integral to this country's history and was especially lauded in nineteenth-

century America, when industrial landscapes were a subcategory of the Hudson River School. George Inness's *Lackawanna Valley*, 1855, springs to mind as the quintessential image celebrating the advancement of industry, as symbolized by a steam locomotive charging through a barren landscape where trees have only recently been removed. Pfahl understood that this conflict—brought to the forefront of our conscience by the problems of nuclear energy—was not newly founded, and he did not intend his photographs to serve as propaganda toward either side of an extremely complex issue.

Pfahl's studies of the picturesque and nineteenth-century American landscape painting, including the starkly beautiful compositions of luminists such as Fitz Hugh Lane and Martin Johnson Heade, emphasized this history. Also of great influence was the pivotal book on the issue, *The Machine in the Garden* by Leo Marx. With references such as the essential pictorial devices of the paintings of the Hudson River School and photos from the era of discovery of the West firmly within his grasp, Pfahl constructed equally magnificent landscape images. Paying keen attention to formal elements, he meticulously composed these referential images, usually photographing them in the atmospheric light of early morning and late afternoon.

The solitude depicted in a Lane painting is dramatically unlike that found in the photographs of *Power Places*; rather than meditative praise of the scene, the stillness of Pfahl's landscapes is filled with suspense. By referring to nineteenth-century compositions and producing beautiful landscape photographs,

Pfahl enhanced the already profound irony of the sumptuous appearance of these locations and the juxtaposition of the functions of the structures now inhabiting them. That these photographs are embraced by both allies and foes of the nuclear power industry attest to their compelling power and beauty.

C.B.

PLATE 42. *Three Mile Island Nuclear Plant*, Susquehanna River, Pennsylvania,
May 1982

PLATE 43. *Peach Bottom Nuclear Plant*, Susquehanna River, Pennsylvania,
September 1982

PLATE 44. *Bruce Mansfield Power Plant*, Ohio River, Pennsylvania, August 1982

PLATE 45. *Niagara Power Project*, Niagara Falls, New York, September 1981

PLATE 46. *Ginna Nuclear Plant*, Lake Ontario, New York, February 1982

PLATE 47. *Indian Point Nuclear Plant*, Hudson River, New York, May 1982

PLATE 48. *Crystal River Nuclear Plant (evening)*, Crystal River, Florida, January 1982

PLATE 49. *Crystal River Nuclear Plant (morning)*, Crystal River, Florida,
January 1982

PLATE 50. *Four Corners Power Plant (evening)*, Farmington, New Mexico,
October 1982

PLATE 51. *Four Corners Power Plant (morning)*, Farmington, New Mexico,
October 1982

PLATE 52. *Navajo Generating Station (morning)*, Lake Powell, Arizona, June 1984

PLATE 53. *Navajo Generating Station (evening)*, Lake Powell, Arizona, June 1984

PLATE 54. *ERB-1 Nuclear Plant*, Big Southern Butte, Idaho, July 1984

PLATE 55. *Pacific Gas and Electric Plant*, Morro Bay, California, June 1983

PLATE 56. *The Geysers Power Plant*, Mayacamas Mountains, California, June 1983

PLATE 57. *Trojan Nuclear Plant*, Columbia River, Oregon, October 1982

PLATE 58. *Idaho Power and Light Plant*, Shoshone Falls, Idaho, July 1984

PLATE 59. *San Onofre Nuclear Generating Station*, San Clemente, California,
June 1981

PLATE 60. *Hoover Dam*, Colorado River, Nevada, June 1983

PLATE 61. *Diablo Dam*, Skagit River, Washington, October 1982

PLATE 62. *Rancho Seco Nuclear Plant*, Sacramento County, California, June 1983

While a visiting professor at the University of New Mexico, Albuquerque, in the 1983–84 academic year, Pfahl participated in a project initiated by Robin Grace and Charles Roitz of the University of Colorado, Boulder. The National Endowment for the Arts Photographic Survey Project, titled "Marks and Measures: Pictographs and Petroglyphs in a Modern Art Context," included the contributions of five photographers whose work preserves the neglected art form. But unlike his colleagues who concentrated on sites where rock drawings could still be found, Pfahl instead composed a series entitled *Submerged Petroglyphs.* The series comprises nine images of reservoirs in New Mexico, each containing a number, beginning with a prefix LA or AR, that hovers within the composition. Pfahl eloquently explains their placement in his introduction to the series, "Elegy for the Drowned," from which excerpts follow:

> These photographs are of that which cannot be seen again. Pecked into smooth black boulders and embellishing large panels of rock, the petroglyphs that lie beneath the waters of New Mexico reservoirs provide a poignant footnote to the history of this most vulnerable form of mark making. . . .
>
> Chance would have it that the first book that came to hand when I arrived in Albuquerque for a year-long visit was *Rock Art in the Cochiti*

Reservoir District, by Polly Schaafsma, with photographs by her husband, Curtis. What a joy to see those many pages filled with little faces, birds and deer, masked serpents, shield-men, and dancing figures! And then, what sadness to realize that I was holding all that remained of these spirited petroglyphs. The book was a report of archaeological salvage activities undertaken before the Rio Grande north of Albuquerque was dammed to form Cochiti Lake. . . .

I felt compelled to revisit the vicinity of these carefully documented sites as a kind of memorial pilgrimage. . . . My choices were already clearly spelled out in precise and technical detail, with site numbers, maps and an accumulation of other data. I had only to get to those vantage points overlooking the submerged archaeological sites and *receive* my picture. The unpredictability of the results of this procedure both intrigued and terrified me. . . .

The site description [of LA 10116] . . . read:
North of LA 10115, a long bench extends for almost a half mile before it is pinched out by steep talus slopes rising directly from the river banks. Petroglyphs were found only at the north end of the bench. . . . A horned serpent and a large anthropomorphic figure, nearly three feet in height, are deeply carved in wide lines in a boulder high in the talus debris. The square body is decorated with lines of dots. The realistic depiction of the feet is unusual among Cochiti Reservoir figures. . . .

As we stood above the silty lake trying to make out the approximate location of the small treasures of LA 10116, we were confronted only with placid swells of opaque water. We shuddered. . . .

Cannot these lost traces of ancient peoples also symbolize *all* the art and civilization, whether along the Nile, in the jungles of the Yucatan, or in the palaces of Venice, destroyed by the pillaging of time, war, progress, or natural disaster? Such were my ever-widening ruminations as I focused on the sad patches of water that betrayed not the slightest sign of the profusion of masks, animals, and tiny handprints submerged below.

C.B./J.P.

PLATE 63. *Abiquiu Reservoir, ". . . large spear points and some feathered shafts"*

PLATE 64. *Abiquiu Reservoir, "Horses and men on horseback . . ."*

PLATE 65. *Cochiti Reservoir, ". . . a masked serpent"*   PLATE 66. *Cochiti Reservoir, ". . . two shield-men"*

PLATE 67. *Cochiti Reservoir, ". . . a phallic male figure"*

PLATE 68. *Cochiti Reservoir, ". . . small man carrying a large shield"*

PLATE 69. *Navajo Reservoir, ". . . horned-winged figure"*   PLATE 70. *Navajo Reservoir, ". . . animals and small hand prints"*

LA 4055

PLATE 71. *Navajo Reservoir, ". . . hand-holding figures"*

There have been subjects so compelling throughout Pfahl's career that the artist has felt obligated to photograph them without knowing their purpose or future format. Rock drawings had sustained his interest in mark-making both before and after his participation in the project from which *Submerged Petroglyphs* resulted. His fascination with nuclear missiles came from finding these objects in the collection at an unusual institution, the National Atomic Museum in Albuquerque. Seduced by the glistening surfaces and riveted patterns formed by their construction, Pfahl set out to photograph details of these missiles and compose abstract images that obscure their origin.

Working simultaneously on both subjects, Pfahl's juxtaposition of transparencies from each on his light table led to their fortuitous, but seemingly inevitable, combination. The personal nature of the ancient rock drawings and the mysterious meanings of their symbols were in stark contrast to the impersonal steel surfaces of the missiles; yet, the formal relationships that Pfahl devised by his purposeful pairing of these images were uncanny.

Attention to both of these subjects provided the artist with his first opportunity to make Cibachrome prints from transparencies. Pfahl found the material to be particularly appropriate for the harsh, metallic qualities he wished to emphasize in rocks and missiles.

Perhaps it is not so surprising after all to find the combination of ancient drawings and obsolete weapons compatible: they are both inadequate means of communication in the contemporary world.

C.B.

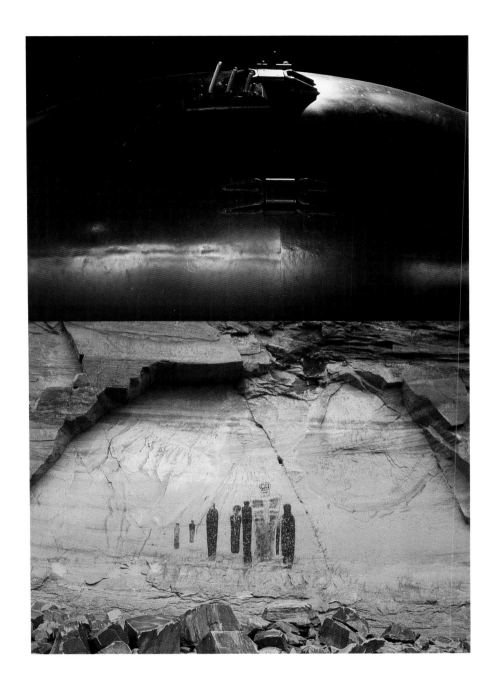

PLATE 72. *Fat Man Atomic Bomb/Great Gallery Pictographs*

PLATE 73. *Redstone Missile/Indian Creek Petroglyphs*

PLATE 74. *Minuteman Missile/Galisteo Basin Petroglyphs*

PLATE 75. *Mark IV ICBM Re-entry Vehicle/Butler Wash Petroglyphs*

PLATE 76. *Terrier Missile Launcher/Butler Wash Petroglyphs*

PLATE 77. *Snark Guided Missile/Horseshoe Canyon Pictographs*

PLATE 78. *Mace Cruise Missile/Sand Island Petroglyphs*

PLATE 79. *B-58 Hustler Pod/Galisteo Basin Petroglyphs*

PLATE 80. *280mm Nuclear Cannon/Galisteo Basin Petroglyphs*

PLATE *81. Bomarc Nuclear Missile/Butler Wash Petroglyphs*

In 1982, a group of Niagara Falls, New York, residents, devoted to the revital-
ization of "community pride and national interest" in the natural wonder so
integral to their lives, organized a committee to plan a celebration of the
centennial anniversary of a publication by Amos W. Sangster (1883–1903).
Sangster, a native of Buffalo, worked for three years on a comprehensive and
heartfelt study that documented the course of the Niagara River. Comprising
fifty full-plate etchings and 103 vignettes, Sangster's detailed account of *The
Niagara River and Falls from Lake Erie to Lake Ontario*, 1886, resulted from
the artist's direct observations of his subject, rather than a reliance on pictorial
formulas typical of the period.

In order to acknowledge the subject of this graphic feat, the Sangster committee intended to commission a contemporary photographer who "would be
sensitive to the working methods and aesthetics of his predecessor." After a
publicized search, the committee's unanimous choice was John Pfahl, who
resided just upstream from the cataract and whose own inquiries into the
picturesque and sublime in landscape photography heightened his interest in
this project. *Arcadia Revisited*, a series of fifty-two color photographs, was the
result of two years of intensive research and exploration of Niagara Falls. The
artist wrote of his many discoveries upon completion of the project:

One of the great personal joys of this photographic odyssey was that it enabled me to experience once again two of my favorite childhood activities: tramping about in the neighborhood fields and forests and fantasizing about time travel. . . .

Before I even began to photograph, I immersed myself in all the historical, geographic, and aesthetic data on the river I could find. I wanted to understand what the Niagara was like a hundred years ago when Amos Sangster trundled his sketchbook from vista to vista. I wanted to know exactly what it was that he and all the other nineteenth-century artists were experiencing and how the conventions and enthusiasms of the day determined the ways in which the concrete reality of rocks, trees, and water were being perceived and transcribed. . . . Would it still be possible to find the nineteenth century lurking in forgotten corners, bypassed by the exigencies of modern times? . . .

To my increasing surprise, the river that I had seen in the old prints and paintings was still very much in place. . . . I spent many exultant hours hiking both the American and Canadian sides of the river and found that almost every vantage point was readily accessible. . . . As I walked along the abandoned Great Gorge trolley line or through the massive boulders of Niagara Glen, I was continually astonished to come across those picturesque vignettes of nature that I had seen while studying prints and paintings. . . . Even the larger panoramas were effortlessly organized into familiar European conventions as if the river, in some time-jumbling way, were the progenitor for all those idyllic schemata that have been passed from one era and continent to the next.

It would have been possible to structure my photographs in such a way that no indicators of the present were discernible. However, I wanted to incorporate into the project as a whole the jostling of time-frames I would feel as I set up my tripod on various rocky promontories. The slow and deliberate process of using a large view camera *en plein air*, waiting hours for revealing conjunctions of light and subject, would often induce a dreamlike state in which my mind would confuse the particulars of the moment with the paradigms of the past. . . .

A nagging problem, and one that I'm not sure can be adequately dealt with photographically, concerns the largely invisible but nevertheless worrisome subtext of environmental pollution. . . . There is an almost unbearable irony to the act of recording an achingly romantic meeting of shadowy forest and luminous water while suffering the stench of untreated sewage dripping nearby. . . .

Perhaps these devastating issues are peripheral to the thrust of this body of work and can best be confronted in other venues, but disquieting thoughts will inevitably figure into the ultimate meaning of these images.

There are still places along the river where one can momentarily forget present-day problems, forget even the past century and the entire panoply of historical time. . . . To stand drenched and awestruck on the rocks under the thundering falls today is to confront again most vividly the great natural force of Niagara that imposed itself as much onto the aesthetics of the nineteenth-century American landscape as on the lay of the land between Lake Erie and Lake Ontario.

C.B./J.P.

PLATE 82. *American Falls from the Cave-of-the-Winds Boardwalk, June 1985*

PLATE 83. *Horseshoe Falls from Below*, September 1985

PLATE 84. *Horseshoe Falls with Spring Ice,* April 1985

PLATE 85. *City of Niagara Falls, New York*, March 1985

PLATE 86. *View Upriver from Under Railroad Bridge,* August 1985

PLATE 87. *Railroad Bridge with Freight Train*, July 1985

PLATE 88. *Two Miles Below the Falls*, August 1985

PLATE 89. *View of the Lower River from Brock's Monument*, July 1985

PLATE 90. *Fort Niagara from Niagara-on-the-Lake*, July 1985

PLATE 91. *Navy Island and Chemical Plants*, April 1985

The intimate knowledge Pfahl gained from his intensive study of the cataract of Niagara for *Arcadia Revisited* only heightened an interest in falling water that had persisted since his youth. As a child, his first painting was of a falls in the Catskill Mountains. Viewing the Niagara brought to mind the hours he spent diverting the paths of streams or escaping to wooded areas as sanctuary. Rediscovering a suite of images by William Henry Jackson (1843–1942) devoted to waterfalls, and a group of reproductions of Japanese woodcuts on the subject, Pfahl's interest was piqued. The challenge was to devise a new means of approaching such a seductive image. The artist found himself to be most fascinated with waterfalls that were somehow unnatural or manipulated for the purposes of industry.

Through his research, Pfahl located guidebooks dating from the nineteenth century that, as expected, described waterfalls distinguished for their potential as an energy source rather than for their inherent beauty. He sought out such designated areas only to find that some no longer existed, while others had been industrialized to the fullest extent possible. Pfahl also located potential sites by talking to residents of areas he was exploring. The expected obstructions that are the result of civilization's intrusion on nature have made some waterfalls impossible to photograph; in other, more accessible, locations, these intrusions became integral elements in the composition.

Pfahl's interest in the land where civilization and the natural world collide has become one of his primary subjects. In the series *Power Places*, for example, the industrial complex is centered in compositions within a natural world made achingly beautiful by the artist's keen sense of place. In *Waterfalls*, Pfahl has composed scenes where an icon of the natural world is the central image. The spectacular light of sunrise and sunset in the Southwest, so essential to the luminist overtones of *Power Places* is absent; instead, Pfahl has incorporated the overcast skies typical of the Northeast to create an image with somber tones, abounding with a sense of age and history. Only occasional highlights of industrial paint are included in these scenes that primarily call up references to the prints and drawings of the nineteenth century.

Using an elongated format, the artist has photographed minor spectacles of nature and willingly included evidence of the constructed intrusions that so frequently surround his subject. *Waterfalls* has become a continuation of Pfahl's exploration of a world that is becoming increasingly unnatural.

C.B.

PLATE 92. *The Great Falls of the Passaic*, Paterson, New Jersey, September 1988

PLATE 93. *Black River Falls*, Watertown, New York, October 1988

PLATE 94. *Upper Genesee Falls*, Rochester, New York, September 1988

PLATE 95. *Ausable River*, Ausable Chasm, New York, October 1988

PLATE 96. *Green Mountain Power Corporation*, Winooski River, Vermont, June 1989

PLATE 97. *Baker's Falls*, Hudson Falls, New York, October 1988

PLATE 98. *Upper Portageville Falls*, Letchworth Park, New York, March 1989

Pfahl's images of smoke are incredibly sumptuous and, at the same time, disturbing and frightening. With this series, he has dared to make one of the extreme hazards of our environment the subject, rather than just an element, of starkly beautiful landscapes left open for interpretation. While the works' titles make clear their origin, their incomparable beauty belies it. The ironic relationship between breathtaking imagery and actual danger becomes literal in this series.

The artist's visual acumen and technical facility are everywhere evident in these prints, some of which are larger than any others to date. Their increased scale suggests an overpowering presence comparable to that of industrial smoke. Although his subject is firmly based in the drama of our physical world, Pfahl's reference to historical origins is readily acknowledged; the inclusion of steam and smoke in images of metropolitan areas at the turn of the century was common. Certainly Stieglitz's evocative and abstract photographs of clouds in the series *Equivalents* also come to mind.

In his own words, the artist describes the experience and power of *Smoke:*

The prodigious display of smoke bursting forth from the stacks of the
Bethlehem Steel coke operation in Lackawanna, New York, can best be

seen from a low slag bluff overlooking the plant from the north. A narrow boat channel of dark water separates me from the silhouetted factory buildings bathed in the radiance of Lake Erie. By the simplest act of looking through the enormous telephoto lens of my Hasselblad, I thrust myself into a phantasmagoria of light and color. Simultaneously attracted and repelled, I feel myself engulfed in a truly awesome spectacle of nature. It is like suddenly being hurled into a roaring cataract, an erupting volcano, or a violent storm at sea. Alarm whistles blow and smoke discharges into the sky, expanding and changing form far more rapidly than I can imagine possible, and at its absolute zenith, dissipating into thin air before I can take another breath.

The presentation has its own geyser-like rhythms and rationale, and fifteen to twenty minutes pass before another discharge takes place. Doubtless, the efficiencies of the internal workings of the mill dictate a logic for the timings, but from my removed vantage point I can only see them as part of an irrational process, terrifying in its capriciousness. Dark, fuming emissions collide with brilliant, white pillows, both swept away in a moment by a thick, yellow vapor. I rotate my camera on its tripod hastily, moving its aim from one vortex of activity to another, trying to keep pace with the rapid transformations. I am grateful when the tempest subsides and I can reload my magazines. I wait again for what seems an interminable time, and just when I impatiently fear that the workmen have closed down the line ending the show for the day, and just when my gaze gets distracted by gulls chasing over the water, the whole process suddenly starts over again. New colors, shapes, and textures arise from other stacks in different hallucinatory combinations.

As the hours pass by and the sun lowers, pink and orange highlights add their glow to the towering clouds of effluvium. Each hour, each day, each time of year holds its own surprises. The plumes on cold mornings are as tight and voluptuous as marble sculpture, but as the day warms, they spread wider in delicate patterns and fragment quickly. Sometimes, when the wind is blowing hard, the smoke billows out in long, horizontal ribbons.

By good fortune, the prevailing winds blow the smoke away from where I like to stand and I can see the dark bundles make their way inland. Occasionally, however, the clouds come right at me and I become immersed in a lung-searing atmosphere of toxicity. I grab at my equipment and stumble back to the car, trying all the while not to inhale too deeply. I recall the recent newspaper stories reporting that this particular plant is first in statewide rankings of highly toxic emissions, discharging 1.4 million tons of benzene alone into the air each year.

Later, at home, it strikes me that the smell of the smoke, overpowering at full strength, is unnervingly familiar to me. In much more dilute form, it wafts by on certain balmy days when I am working in the garden. I am hardly conscious of it. It is one of the many familiar aromas, along with the newly turned earth and the freshly cut grass, that I have come to identify with the notion of home.

C.B./J.P.

PLATE 99. *Bethlehem #16*, Lackawanna, NY 1988

PLATE 100. *Goodyear #5*, Niagara Falls, NY 1989

PLATE 101. *Bethlehem #22*, Lackawanna, NY 1988

PLATE 102. *Bethlehem #158*, Lackawanna, NY 1989

PLATE 103. *Bethlehem #153*, Lackawanna, NY 1989

PLATE 104. *Bethlehem #41*, Lackawanna, NY 1988

PLATE 105. *Bethlehem #79*, Lackawanna, NY 1988

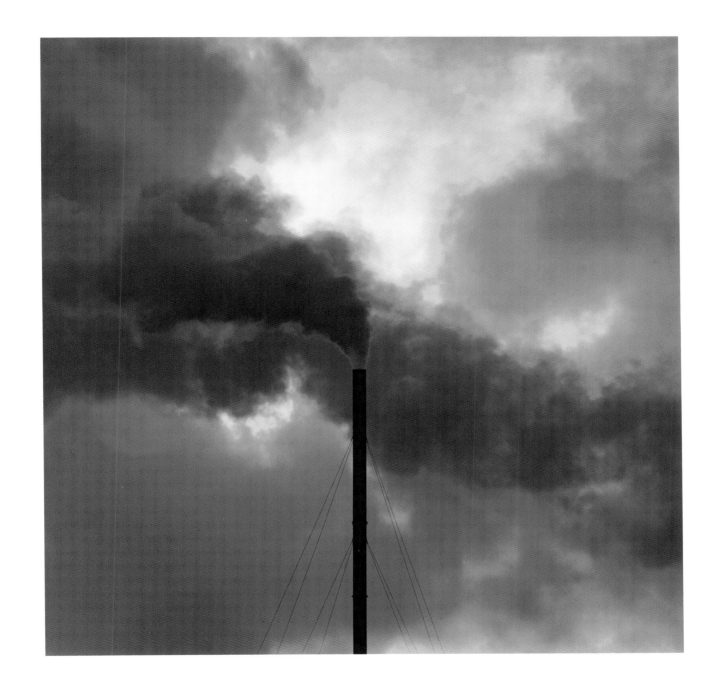

PLATE 106. *O-Cel-O #7*, Tonawanda, NY 1989

1939   Born in New York, New York, to Hans and Anna Pfahl, recent immigrants from Germany.

1942   Family moves to Wanaque, New Jersey.

1944   Receives first camera, a "Baby Brownie."

1945   Brother Walter is born.

Pfahl recalls that his childhood is "normal and happy"; he attends public schools; social gatherings stem from family's participation in a hiking club that plans outings in the Catskills as well as more distant locations. Of note is an extended trip to upstate New York in 1951 that includes stops at Watkins Glen, Letchworth State Park, and Niagara Falls. Travels are regularly documented by Pfahl.

1951   Receives first 35mm camera, a Voightlander.

1955   Attends *The Family of Man* exhibition at the Museum of Modern Art, New York, which he recalls as a memorable experience.

1957   Graduates from Butler High School, New Jersey.

Enters Syracuse University, New York, majoring in graphic design; professors include Bauhaus-educated M. Peter Pienning, professor of advertising design,

From the artist's scrapbook of a family trip
to Niagara Falls, 1951.

and Fred A. Demarest, professor of photography, who initiated the first course in photography in conjunction with the School of Communications, which Pfahl enthusiastically attends. Joins an outing club, where he first meets Bonnie Gordon, whom he would later marry.

1958   Works during summer at Mohonk Mountain House, a resort in the Shawan-gunk Mountains, New Paltz, New York. The Victorian setting—where nature is subtly manipulated in order to be more carefully appreciated by the visitor—strongly influences Pfahl's vision.

1959   Visits the West for the first time, working at Jackson Lake Lodge in the Grand Tetons during the summers of 1959 and 1960. Continues to photograph, now with a Rolleiflex.

1961   Receives bachelor of fine arts degree in graphic design from Syracuse University; travels to Europe, visiting England, France, Spain, Switzerland, Germany, Holland, and Denmark.

Color printing in one's own darkroom becomes possible and Pfahl attempts his first Type-C prints. Images include details from nature such as lichen on rocks.

1961–63   Is inducted into the United States Army and stationed in Fort Belvoir, Virginia. Works as a draftsman in an engineering battalion.

1964   Returns to New York and looks for a job in the field of photography. Becomes assistant to commercial photographer Paul Elfenbein; acquires first Nikon with interchangeable lenses. Also views an exhibition of the work of Harry

Callahan at the Hallmark Gallery and later contacts Callahan. Dissatisfied with working conditions, leaves Elfenbein studio for California.

1965   Drives to Los Angeles with brother and works for commercial photographer Herbert Bruce Cross, at whose studio he spends most of his time developing black-and-white prints. Makes the ritual pilgrimage to Carmel, California, to visit Ansel Adams and is received by Adams and Nancy Newhall, who view his work; images include a variety of subjects. Dissatisfied with his experiences in commercial photography, calls Demarest, who is originating a graduate program in photography at Syracuse University. Before returning to the East, marries Bonnie Gordon and travels with her to Mexico, where he completes his first sustained body of work, focusing on Oaxaca.

1966   Receives graduate assistantship at Syracuse University and attends the School of Communication in order to study photography, enrolling in classes that are recognized as the first in color photography at the graduate level in the United States. Studies primarily with Demarest and Thomas Richards; also attends course on the history of photography conducted by Gerda Peterich, who instills in him a love of the subject. Regularly visits New York and Rochester, New York, to view exhibitions.

1968   Receives master's degree from School of Communication, Syracuse University, and immediately joins faculty of Rochester Institute of Technology, New York, as instructor in the School of Photographic Arts and Sciences.

1969   Begins to develop three-dimensional, molded plastic forms on which he has screenprinted images of clouds, trees, waves, and other details from the natural world. The works are hung from the ceiling or mounted on a wall either singly or in groups of repeated shapes.

Travels to Scotland in summer.

1970   First exhibition of three-dimensional, screenprinted works at the Schuman Gallery, Rochester.

1972   Conducts photography workshop at Penland School of Arts and Crafts, North Carolina; also in 1974, 1975, 1976, and 1977. Among other artists he meets there are Nathan Lyons, Emmett Gowin, Henry Holmes Smith, and Evon Streetman. Moves to Buffalo in September and commutes to Rochester on a weekly basis.

Work is included in *60's Continuum* at International Museum of Photography at George Eastman House, Rochester.

1974   Publishes *Piles* (Rochester: Visual Studies Workshop), a limited edition "pop-up" book comprising screenprinted photographic images of piles of various materials.

1975   During his residency at Penland in June, Pfahl begins the series *Altered Landscapes*; travels to Bermuda in August and photographs images for that series; also in residence at Artpark in Lewiston, New York, in August.

Recipient of New York State Creative Artists Public Service Grant.

1976   In March, travels to Death Valley and California, and to North Carolina in April, in order to find suitable landscapes for his series.

Recipient of artist's grant in photography from National Endowment for the
Arts.

Visual Studies Workshop, Rochester. First exhibition of the ongoing series
Altered Landscapes.

1977 In February, travels to Florida; in August and September, to Colorado, Utah,
and Wyoming; and in October, to Utah and New Mexico.

Attends workshop *Photography and Aspects of the Mimetic Tradition*, conducted by William E. Parker at Visual Studies Workshop, which gives him
new philosophical underpinnings for much future work.

1978 In March, travels to California, Hawaii, Utah, and Colorado, completing
Altered Landscapes. Lectures at national conference of Society for Photographic Education in Asilomar, California.

In November, lectures at Massachusetts Institute of Technology Creative
Photography Lab in Cambridge.

Robert Freidus Gallery, New York, exhibits *John Pfahl: Photographs of Altered
Landscapes.*

1979 In February and March, travels to Florida and begins to work intensively on
Picture Windows; travels to Washington, Idaho, Montana, and Wyoming in
August.

Work is included in the circulating exhibition *Fabricated to Be Photo-*

graphed, San Francisco Museum of Modern Art, and *American Photography in the 70's* at the Art Institute of Chicago.

1980   Continues work on *Picture Windows*. From February through June is artist-in-residence at the Sun Valley Center for Arts and Humanities in Idaho, and travels to Utah and New Mexico; travels to Colorado in August and to California in December.

Work is included in exhibition *Reasoned Space* at Center for Creative Photography, University of Arizona, Tucson.

1981   Travels to California in June and photographs San Onofre Nuclear Power Plant, which would become the first image in the series *Power Places*. Attends workshop on platinum/palladium printing process at Visual Studies Workshop, Rochester, in summer and uses technique in series *Video Landscapes* in the winter months.

Work is included in exhibition *The New Color: A Decade of Color Photography* at the Everson Museum, Syracuse.

Altered Landscapes: The Photographs of John Pfahl, with introduction by Peter C. Bunnell, is published by Friends of Photography.

1982   Concentrates on photographing for *Power Places*; travels to Colorado in March; to North Carolina, South Carolina, and Pennsylvania in August and September; to New Mexico, Washington, Oregon, and Minnesota in October.

Work is included in circulating exhibition *Color as Form: A History of Color*

Photography at the International Museum of Photography at George Eastman House, Rochester.

1983   Continues visiting power plants in California in June; resigns from Rochester Institute of Technology; appointed visiting professor at University of New Mexico, Albuquerque, for academic year 1983–84.

1984   Travels throughout New Mexico, Arizona, Utah, and Idaho, photographing for the series *Power Places;* also participates in National Endowment for the Arts Photographic Survey Project "Marks and Measures: Pictographs and Petroglyphs in a Modern Art Context" and composes *Submerged Petroglyphs;* also photographs rock drawings and missiles and later combines these images in series *Missile/Glyphs.*

Los Angeles County Museum of Art exhibits *Power Places.* Submits proposal to Sangster Committee, Niagara Falls, for a project in which he would document the Niagara River from Lake Erie to Lake Ontario. The committee unanimously approves of Pfahl's proposal.

1985   Begins work on series of photographs that will be part of *Arcadia Revisited: Niagara River and Falls from Lake Erie to Lake Ontario.*

Work is included in *American Images, 1945–1980* at the Barbican Gallery, London.

Work is included in the circulating exhibition *Images of Excellence* at the International Museum of Photography at George Eastman House, Rochester.

John Pfahl, 1987.

1986   Continues to work on *Arcadia Revisited;* the first images are exhibited at Buscaglia-Castellani Art Gallery of Niagara University, Niagara Falls, New York.

1987   International Museum of Photography at George Eastman House, Rochester, exhibits *Power Places.*

        Picture Windows, with an introduction by Edward Bryant, is published by New York Graphic Society; Little, Brown and Company.

1988   Travels to West Germany and Austria in July; lectures in Frankfurt, Offenbach, and Essen, West Germany.

        Fotografie Forum Frankfurt exhibits four series of work in a show entitled *John Pfahl.*

        Visual Studies Workshop Gallery, Rochester, exhibits *Arcadia Revisited.*

        Arcadia Revisited: The Niagara River from Lake Erie to Lake Ontario, with texts by Estelle Jussim and Anthony Bannon, is published by the University of New Mexico Press in association with the Buscaglia-Castellani Art Gallery, Niagara Falls, New York.

        Travels to Adirondack Mountains to photograph waterfalls. Begins photographing *Smoke* series.

1989   Work is included in exhibition *On the Art of Fixing a Shadow: One Hundred and Fifty Years of Photography* at the National Gallery of Art, Washington, D.C., and the Art Institute of Chicago.

FRONTISPIECE. *International Paper Company (formerly "The Great Falls of the Hudson")*, Corinth, New York, October 1988, from *Waterfalls*, 1988–

Altered Landscapes, 1974–78; 1980

Ektacolor prints
8 × 10 in. and 16 × 20 in.

1. *Moonrise over Pie Pan*, Capitol Reef National Park, Utah, October 1977

2. *Music I*, Ellicottville, New York, May 1974

3. *Pink Rock Rectangle*, Artpark, Lewiston, New York, August 1975

4. *Blue Right-angle*, Albright-Knox Art Gallery, Buffalo, New York, September 1975

5. *Double Diamond*, Penland, North Carolina, June 1975

6. *Red Setters in Red Field*, Charlotte, North Carolina, April 1976

7. *Red Arrow*, Roan Mountain, North Carolina, June 1975

8. *Shed with Blue Dotted Lines*, Penland, North Carolina, June 1975

9. *Marsh Grass and Hammock*, Pine Island, Florida, February 1977

10. *Australian Pines*, Fort DeSoto, Florida, February 1977

11. *Triangle*, Bermuda, August 1975

12. *Net and Ship*, "The Sophia," Boston, Massachusetts, June 1978

13. *Wave, Lave, Lace*, Pescadero Beach, California, March 1978

14. *Canyon Point*, Zion National Park, Utah, October 1977

15. *Rock Opening*, Big Sur, California, December 1980

16. *Moose and Arrow*, Grand Teton National Park, Wyoming, September 1977

17. *The Grand Teton with Dotted Line*, Grand Teton National Park, Wyoming, August 1977

18. *Geological Demarcations*, Garden of the Gods, Colorado Springs, Colorado, August 1977

19. *Slanting Orange Lines*, Hell's Half Acre, Wyoming, September 1977

20. *Great Salt Lake Angles*, Great Salt Lake, Utah, October 1977

Picture Windows, 1978–81

Ektacolor prints
20 × 24 in. and 16 × 20 in.

21. *11000 SW 57th Avenue, Miami, Florida*, March 1979

22. *1901 NW 55th Terrace, Gainesville, Florida*, March 1979

23. *1390 South Dixie Highway, Coral Gables, Florida*, March 1979

24. *797 Potomac Avenue, Buffalo, New York*, September 1981

25. *Pingry Hill Road, Andover, New York*, October 1979

26. *228 Grant Avenue, San Francisco, California*, December 1980

27. *Boots Brown Drive, Gimlet, Idaho*, March 1980

28. *One Alpenrose Drive, Ketchum, Idaho*, April 1980

29. *Garden of the Gods Loop Drive, Colorado Springs, Colorado*, July 1980

30. *Kaanapali Coast, Maui, Hawaii*, March 1978

Video Landscapes, 1981

Platinum/palladium prints
14 × 11 in. (paper)

31. *PFV-1-A / Knot's Landing / CBS-TV*

32. *PFV-2-A / Fantasy Island / ABC-TV*

33. *PFV-3-A / Masterpiece Theater: Sunset Song / PBS-TV*

34. *PFV-7-A / Masterpiece Theater: Therese Raquin / PBS-TV*

35. *PFV-12-B / Shock of the New: The View from the Edge / PBS-TV*

36. *PFV-14-D / Sunday Morning: Storm Over Paradise / CBS-TV*

37. *PFV-4-A / Mastercard Traveler Cheques / CBS-TV*

38. *PFV-15-D / American Odyssey / PBS-TV*

39. *PFV-13-A / National Parks: Playground or Paradise / PBS-TV*

40. *PFV-9-A / Etosha: Place of Dry Water / PBS-TV*

41. *PFV-15-A / American Odyssey / PBS-TV*

Power Places, 1981–84

Ektacolor prints
16 × 20 in.

42. *Three Mile Island Nuclear Plant*, Susquehanna River, Pennsylvania, May 1982

43. *Peach Bottom Nuclear Plant*, Susquehanna River, Pennsylvania, September 1982

44. *Bruce Mansfield Power Plant*, Ohio River, Pennsylvania, August 1982

45. *Niagara Power Project*, Niagara Falls, New York, September 1981

46. *Ginna Nuclear Plant*, Lake Ontario, New York, February 1982

47. *Indian Point Nuclear Plant*, Hudson River, New York, May 1982

48. *Crystal River Nuclear Plant (evening)*, Crystal River, Florida, January 1982

49. *Crystal River Nuclear Plant (morning)*, Crystal River, Florida, January 1982

50. *Four Corners Power Plant (evening)*, Farmington, New Mexico, October 1982

51. *Four Corners Power Plant (morning)*, Farmington, New Mexico, October 1982

52. *Navajo Generating Station (morning)*, Lake Powell, Arizona, June 1984

53. *Navajo Generating Station (evening)*, Lake Powell, Arizona, June 1984

54. *ERB-1 Nuclear Plant*, Big Southern Butte, Idaho, July 1984

55. *Pacific Gas and Electric Plant*, Morro Bay, California, June 1983

56. *The Geysers Power Plant*, Mayacamas Mountains, California, June 1983

57. *Trojan Nuclear Plant*, Columbia River, Oregon, October 1982

58. *Idaho Power and Light Plant*, Shoshone Falls, Idaho, July 1984

59. *San Onofre Nuclear Generating Station*, San Clemente, California, June 1981

60. *Hoover Dam*, Colorado River, Nevada, June 1983

61. *Diablo Dam*, Skagit River, Washington, October 1982

62. *Rancho Seco Nuclear Plant*, Sacramento County, California, June 1983

Submerged Petroglyphs, 1984

Ektacolor prints

14 × 11 in.

63. *Abiquiu Reservoir, ". . . large spear points and some feathered shafts"*

64. *Abiquiu Reservoir, "Horses and men on horseback . . ."*

65. *Cochiti Reservoir, ". . . a masked serpent"*

66. *Cochiti Reservoir, ". . . two shield-men"*

67. *Cochiti Reservoir, ". . . a phallic male figure"*

68. *Cochiti Reservoir, ". . . small man carrying a large shield"*

69. *Navajo Reservoir, ". . . horned-winged figure"*

70. *Navajo Reservoir, ". . . animals and small hand prints"*

71. *Navajo Reservoir, ". . . hand-holding figures"*

Missile/Glyphs, 1984–85

Each two Cibachrome prints, 31 × 22 in. on aluminum panel

72. *Fat Man Atomic Bomb/Great Gallery Pictographs*

73. *Redstone Missile/Indian Creek Petroglyphs*

74. *Minuteman Missile/Galisteo Basin Petroglyphs*

75. *Mark IV ICBM Re-entry Vehicle/Butler Wash Petroglyphs*

76. *Terrier Missile Launcher/Butler Wash Petroglyphs*

77. *Snark Guided Missile/Horseshoe Canyon Pictographs*

78. *Mace Cruise Missile/Sand Island Petroglyphs*

79. *B-58 Hustler Pod/Galisteo Basin Petroglyphs*

80. *280mm Nuclear Cannon/Galisteo Basin Petroglyphs*

81. *Bomarc Nuclear Missile/Butler Wash Petroglyphs*

Arcadia Revisited, 1985–87

Ektacolor prints

16 × 20 in.

82. *American Falls from the Cave-of-the-Winds Boardwalk,* June 1985

83. *Horseshoe Falls from Below,* September 1985

84. *Horseshoe Falls with Spring Ice,* April 1985

85. *City of Niagara Falls, New York,* March 1985

86. *View Upriver from Under Railroad Bridge*, August 1985

87. *Railroad Bridge with Freight Train*, July 1985

88. *Two Miles Below the Falls*, August 1985

89. *View of the Lower River from Brock's Monument*, July 1985

90. *Fort Niagara from Niagara-on-the-Lake*, July 1985

91. *Navy Island and Chemical Plants*, April 1985

Waterfalls, 1988–

Ektacolor prints
24 × 30 in.

92. *The Great Falls of the Passaic*, Paterson, New Jersey, September 1988

93. *Black River Falls*, Watertown, New York, October 1988

94. *Upper Genesee Falls*, Rochester, New York, September 1988

95. *Ausable River*, Ausable Chasm, New York, October 1988

96. *Green Mountain Power Corporation*, Winooski River, Vermont, June 1989

97. *Baker's Falls*, Hudson Falls, New York, October 1988

98. *Upper Portageville Falls*, Letchworth Park, New York, March 1989

Smoke, 1988–

Ektacolor prints
20 × 20 in. and 30 × 30 in.

99. *Bethlehem #16*, Lackawanna, NY 1988

100. *Goodyear #5*, Niagara Falls, NY 1989

101. *Bethlehem #22*, Lackawanna, NY 1988

102. *Bethlehem #158*, Lackawanna, NY 1989

103. *Bethlehem #153*, Lackawanna, NY 1989

104. *Bethlehem #41*, Lackawanna, NY 1988

105. *Bethlehem #79*, Lackawanna, NY 1988

106. *O-Cel-O #7*, Tonawanda, NY 1989

By the Artist

Books and Reviews

1980   *John Pfahl: Altered Landscapes.* Essay by William E. Parker. Sun Valley, Idaho: Sun Valley Center for the Arts and Humanities, 1980.

1981   *Altered Landscapes: The Photographs of John Pfahl.* Introduction by Peter C. Bunnell. New York: Friends of Photography in association with Robert Freidus Gallery, 1981.

   Bennett, Derek. "John Pfahl: Altered Landscapes." *European Photography* (Göttingen, West Germany), Apr.–June 1982, pp. 34–35.

   Garner, Gretchen. "Reviews." *Exposure 19:4*, Journal of the Society for Photographic Education (Albuquerque), 1981, p. 43.

   Wilcox, Beth. "Altered Landscapes." *Photo Communiqué* (Toronto), Winter 1981/82, p. 33.

1982   *Altered Landscapes: The Photographs of John Pfahl.* New York: RFG Publishing, Inc., 1982.

1987   *Picture Windows.* Introduction by Edward Bryant. Boston: New York Graphic Society, Little, Brown and Company, 1987.

   Averkieff, Irina. "The Allure of the Landscape." *Los Angeles Times*, Dec. 6, 1987.

   Chon, Richard. "Pictures are Window on World." *Buffalo News*, Nov. 15, 1987, pp. G1, G4.

   Garner, Gretchen. *Booklist* (Chicago), Jan. 15, 1988.

   Goss, Barbara. "Books for the Coffee Table." *Syracuse New Times*, Feb. 10, 1988.

   Grundberg, Andy. "Book Review: Photography." *The New York Times*, Dec. 6, 1987, p. 20.

   Piperato, Susan. "Windows to the World." *Popular Photography*, Mar. 1988, pp. 64–67.

1988   *Arcadia Revisited: Niagara River and Falls from Lake Erie to Lake Ontario.* Essays by Estelle Jussim and Anthony Bannon. Albuquerque: Buscaglia-Castellani Art Gallery of Niagara University and the University of New Mexico Press, 1988.

On the Artist

General Books

1978   *Dumont Foto Yearbook* (Cologne), Oct. 1978.

1979   *Time-Life Yearbook 1979.* New York: Time-Life Books, 1979.

1980   *American Photographs: 1970 to 1980.* Bellingham, Wash.: Washington Art Consortium, 1980, p. 74.

Coke, Van Deren. *Fabricated to be Photographed.* San Francisco: San Francisco Museum of Modern Art, 1980.

Upton, Barbara, and John Upton. *Photography.* Boston: Little Brown and Company, 1980.

1981   *Aspekte Amerikanischer Farbfotographie.* Hanover, West Germany: Kunstmuseum Hannover, 1981.

Cahn, Robert, and Robert Glenn Ketchum. *American Photographers and the National Parks.* New York: Viking Press, 1981.

New American Colour Photography. London: Institute of Contemporary Arts, 1981.

Time-Life Yearbook 1981. New York: Time-Life Books, 1981.

1983   *The Gallery of World Photography: Photograph as Fine Art.* New York: E. P. Dutton, 1983.

Green, Jonathan. *A Critical History of American Photography.* New York: Harry N. Abrams, 1983.

1984   Eauclaire, Sally. *New Color/New Work.* New York: Abbeville Press, 1984.

Jussim, Estelle, and Elizabeth Lindquist-Cock. *Landscape as Photograph.* New Haven: Yale University Press, 1984.

Landscape. Preface by David Plowden, introduction by Ian Jeffrey. London: Thames and Hudson, 1984.

1985   Gauss, Kathleen McCarthy. *New American Photography.* Los Angeles: Los Angeles County Museum of Art, 1985.

1986   Heiting, Manfred, ed. *50. Jahre Moderne Farbfotographie 1936–1986.* Cologne: Messe-und Austellungs-Ges., 1986.

Le Magny, Jean-Claude, and André Rouille. *Histoire de la Photographie.* Paris: Editions Bordas, 1986.

North, Ian. *International Photography 1920–1980.* Canberra: Australian National Gallery, 1986.

1987   Alinder, James G., ed. *Light Years.* Carmel, Calif.: Friends of Photography, 1987.

1988   *Marks in Place: Contemporary Responses to Rock Art.* Photographs by Linda Connor, Rick Dingus, Steve Fitch, John Pfahl,

Charles Roitz; essays by Polly Schaafsma and Keith Davis; foreword by Lucy R. Lippard. Albuquerque: University of New Mexico Press, 1988.

Weishaus, Joel. "Marks in Place: Contemporary Responses to Rock Art." *Artspace* (Albuquerque), Spring 1988, pp. 8–12.

Selected Articles

1976   Uzemack, E. M. "Non-Traditional Imagery." *Midwest Art* (Milwaukee), May 1976, p. 14.

1978   Grundberg, Andy. "Photos That Lie." *Modern Photography* (New York), May 1978, pp. 102–4.

Scully, Julia. "Seeing Pictures." *Modern Photography* (New York), Mar. 1978.

"Shows We've Seen." *Popular Photography* (Los Angeles), Oct. 1978.

Willig, Nancy Tobin. "John Pfahl's Photography, Variations on the Landscape." *Buffalo Courier Express*, Nov. 26, 1978, pp. 12–13; 15–16.

1979   Bannon, Anthony. "John Pfahl's Picturesque Paradoxes." *Afterimage* (Rochester, N.Y.), Feb. 1979, pp. 10–13.

Grundberg, Andy. "Not Just Pretty Pictures." *Soho Weekly News* (New York), Apr. 26, 1979.

"John Pfahl." *Rocky Mountain Magazine* (Denver), June 1979, pp. 51–55.

Lynch, David E. "Second Lady's Buffalo Art Goes on Display." *Buffalo Courier Express*, Apr. 5, 1979, p. 4.

Murray, Joan. "Fabricated for the Camera." *Artweek* (Oakland, Calif.), Dec. 8, 1979, pp. 11–12.

"Pfahl on Color." *Wisconsin Photographer* (Milwaukee), Nov. 1979.

1980   Grundberg, Andy. "Gone with the Window." *Soho Weekly News* (New York), Oct. 8, 1980.

"John Pfahl." *Print Collector's Newsletter* (New York), Jan.–Feb. 1980, p. 202.

Bannon, Anthony. "New Art." *Buffalo News*, Jan. 18, 1981, p. F1.

Pelissero, Lauri. "Photography on the Block." *AirCal Magazine* (Laguna Beach, Calif.), Oct. 1981, pp. 40–45.

1982   Davis, Keith, and William Kay. "A Conversation with John Pfahl." *Exposure 20:3*, Journal of the Society for Photographic Education, 1982, pp. 6–11.

Davis, Keith, and William Kay. "Conversation with John Pfahl." *Forum*, Kansas City Artists Coalition (Kansas City), May 1982, pp. 5–6.

Nilson, Lisbet. "Pictures at an Exhibition." *Metropolitan Home*, Feb. 1982, pp. 39–44.

"Subterranean Art." *Buffalo Courier Express*, Aug. 3, 1982, p. A10.

1983   Bannon, Anthony. "Review: Art—Looking Down the Tracks at Subway Art." *Buffalo News*, May 20, 1983, *Gusto*, p. 16.

Rome, Stuart. "John Pfahl Interview." *Northlight*, University of Arizona (Tempe), vol. 14, 1983, pp. 34–41.

1984   Bright, Deborah. "Pfahl's 'Power Places' Defused." *New Art Examiner* (Chicago), Feb. 1984, p. 29.

Chamberlain, Ann. "The Expression of Size." *The Exploratorium* (San Francisco), Summer 1984, pp. 22–26.

Langer, Freddy. "Pfahl in der Natur." *Frankfurter Allgemeine Magazin* (Frankfurt), Apr. 13, 1984, pp. 24–31.

1985   Bannon, Anthony. "Windows Are Portals to the Past." *Buffalo News*, May 12, 1985, p. E5.

Davis, Douglas. "Seeing Isn't Believing." *Newsweek* (New York), June 3, 1985, pp. 69–70.

1987   Heegen, Rolf. "Zwischen Natur und Technik: Skulpturen der Kraft." *Frankfurter Allgemeine Magazin* (Frankfurt), Apr. 1987, pp. 86–92.

Morgan, Robert C. "Mistaken Documents: Photography and Conceptual Art." *CEPA Quarterly* (Buffalo), pp. 10–11.

1988   Cardinale, Anthony. "Art and Soul." *Buffalo News Magazine*, Jan. 17, 1988, pp. 6–17, 25.

F.A.Z. "Der Strich in der Landschaft." *Stadtteil* (Frankfurt), July 11, 1988, p. 31.

Selected One-Artist Exhibitions and Reviews

1973   East Tennessee State University, Johnson City.

1976   Visual Studies Workshop Gallery, Rochester, New York. *Altered Landscapes*, May 28–July 30.

1978   MFA Gallery, Rochester Institute of Technology, New York. *John Pfahl: Recent Color Photographs*, Oct. 25–Nov. 4.

Nina Freudenheim Gallery, Buffalo, New York. *Altered Landscapes*, Sept. 26–Oct. 26.

Bannon, Anthony. "The Altered Landscapes of John Pfahl." *Buffalo Evening News*, Sept. 24, 1978, pp. G1–G2.

Kline, Katy. "Art Review: Freudenheim Exhibits Provocative." *Buffalo Courier Express*, Sept. 29, 1978.

Phoenix Art Museum. *John Pfahl Photographs*, Apr. 19–May 28.

Picker Art Gallery, Colgate University, Hamilton, New York. *Photographs of Altered Landscapes*, Nov. 11–Dec. 9.

"Colgate Hosts Art Exhibits." *Syracuse*, Nov. 8, 1978, p. H9.

Yung, Susan. "Golub and Pfahl Present Works." *Colgate Maroon* (Hamilton, N.Y.), Nov. 7, 1978.

Princeton University Art Museum, New Jersey. *John Pfahl: Photographs of Altered Landscapes*, Mar. 14–Apr. 23.

Robert Freidus Gallery, New York. *John Pfahl: Photographs of Altered Landscapes*, Feb. 7–Mar. 4.

Euclaire, Sally. "His Forte: Fooling the Eye." *Democrat and Chronicle* (Rochester, N.Y.), Feb. 5, 1978, p. 1E.

Lifson, Ben. "You Can Fool Some of the Eyes Some of the Time." *The Village Voice* (New York), Mar. 9, 1978, p. 68.

Tatransky, Valentin. "John Pfahl." *Arts Magazine* (New York), Apr. 1978, p. 29.

St. Lawrence University, Canton, New York.

State University of New York at Oneonta.

Thomas Segal Gallery, Boston. *John Pfahl Color Photographs*, Nov. 11–Dec. 6.

1979   Bard College, Hudson, New York.

Fort Steilacoom Community College, Tacoma, Washington.

Madison Art Center, Wisconsin.

Robert Freidus Gallery, New York. *John Pfahl: Recent Photographs*, Apr. 24–June 2.

    Grundberg, Andy. "John Pfahl: Robert Freidus Gallery." *Soho Weekly News* (New York), May 17, 1979, p. 48.

    Olejarz, Harold. "John Pfahl." *Arts Magazine* (New York), Sept. 1979, p. 29.

University of Massachusetts at Amherst. *John Pfahl*, Nov. 6–Dec. 16.

1980   Bell Gallery, Brown University, Providence, Rhode Island. *John Pfahl: Photographs of Altered Landscapes*, Jan. 4–25.

    "Images that get ideas across." *Providence Journal*, Jan. 6, 1980.

    Peters, Marsha. "Shows: John Pfahl and Al Souza." *Views, A New England Journal of Photography* (Boston), Spring 1980, p. 22.

Colorado Mountain College, Breckenridge. July 19–Aug. 7.

Delahunty Gallery, Dallas.

Dibden Gallery, Johnson State College, Vermont. *John Pfahl—Altered Landscapes.*

Jeb Gallery, Providence, Rhode Island.

Kathleen Ewing Gallery, Washington, D.C.

Paul Cava Gallery, Philadelphia. *Color Photographs*, Feb. 22–Mar. 22.

Robert Freidus Gallery, New York. *John Pfahl—Picture Windows*, Sept. 9–Oct. 11.

Sun Valley Center Gallery, Sun Valley Center for the Arts and Humanities, Idaho. *John Pfahl*, Mar. 21–Apr. 30.

Visual Studies Workshop Gallery, Rochester, New York. *John Pfahl—Picture Windows*, Sept. 9–Oct. 11.

    Eauclaire, Sally. "John Pfahl at the Visual Studies Workshop and Robert Freidus." *Art in America* (New York), Sept. 1981, p. 159.

    Rice, Shelley. "John Pfahl." *Artforum* (New York), Nov. 1980, p. 88.

1981   The Art Gallery at Harbourfront, Toronto, Canada. *Window Series*, Oct. 9–Nov. 1.

The Burton Gallery of Photographic Art, Toronto, Canada. *John Pfahl Altered Landscapes*, June 6–July 1.

The Friends of Photography Gallery, Carmel, California. *Color Photographs by John Pfahl*, Apr. 10–May 10.

Grapestake Gallery, San Francisco. *Picture Windows*, Mar. 29–Apr. 25.

New Gallery, Cleveland. *John Pfahl: Color Photographs*, Feb. 27–Mar. 28.

New Image Gallery, James Madison University, Harrisonburg, Virginia. *John Pfahl*, Jan. 12–30.

Nina Freudenheim Gallery, Buffalo, New York. *Picture Windows*, Jan. 31–Mar. 6.

Bannon, Anthony. "Artists Engage the Eye, Then Delight the Mind." *Buffalo News*, Feb. 6, 1981, p. 30.

Bannon, Anthony. "New Art: In the glow of international success, Charles Clough and John Pfahl exhibit in Nina Freudenheim Gallery." *Buffalo News*, Jan. 18, 1981, p. 71.

Huntington, Richard. "Pfahl Seen as the Ultimate Guide." *Buffalo Courier Express*, Feb.17, 1981, p. 19.

Pierce Street Gallery, Birmingham, Michigan.

Susan Spiritus Gallery, Newport Beach, California. *John Pfahl: Picture Windows*, Feb. 7–Mar. 7.

Johnstone, Mark. "Nostalgic Places and Ambiguous Spaces." *Artweek* (Oakland, Calif.), Feb. 28, 1981, p. 16.

Thomas Segal Gallery, Boston. *Altered Landscapes*.

Thomas Segal Gallery, Boston. *New Color Photographs—Picture Windows*, Jan. 10–Feb. 4.

1982   Film-in-the-Cities Gallery, St. Paul. *Picture Windows*, Apr. 4–28.

Tortue Gallery, Santa Monica, California.

1983   Adriana Milla Gallery, Milan, Italy. *Paesaggi alterati*.

Somaini, Luisa. "Paesaggio con fili e pizzi." *La Reppublica Milano*, Mar. 23, 1983.

Turroni, Giuseppe. "Fotografia John Pfahl: 'L'occhio' saggio. *Corriere della Sera* (Milan), Mar. 27, 1983.

Contemporary Arts Center, New Orleans. *Altered Landscapes*, Jan. 9–Feb. 13.

Green, Robert. "CAC photo-show entries stress both form, content." *The Times-Picayune* (New Orleans), Jan. 30, 1983, Sec. 3, p. 4.

Freidus/Ordover Gallery, New York. *Power Places*, Sept. 23–Oct. 19.

Edwards, Owen. "Exhibitions: The Comment of No Comment." *American Photographer* (New York), Oct. 1983, pp. 32–34.

Handy, Ellen. "John Pfahl." *Arts Magazine* (New York), Dec. 1983, p. 38.

"Power Places." *Electric Perspectives* (Washington, D.C.), Spring 1984, pp. 24–27.

The Museum of Contemporary Photography, Columbia College, Chicago. *Power Places*, Oct. 21–Dec. 2.

Sheldon Memorial Art Gallery, Lincoln, Nebraska.

1984   The Camera Obscura Gallery, Denver, Colorado. *John Pfahl: Power Places*, Sept. 14–Oct. 28.

Film/Gallery, Center for Contemporary Arts, Santa Fe, New Mexico. *John Pfahl: Nineteenth Century Video Landscapes*, Mar. 14–Apr. 14, 1984.

Jones Troyer Gallery, Washington, D.C. *Two Portfolios: The Altered Landscape and Power Places*, June 30–July 21.

La Jolla Museum of Contemporary Art, California. *John Pfahl—Power Places*, Jan. 21–Mar. 4.

Damsker, Matt. "On Photography: John Pfahl's Power Politics." *Los Angeles Times*, Feb. 12, 1984, p. 99ff.

Lugo, Mark-Elliott. "Images of landscape, power brought into focus." *The Tribune* (San Diego), Jan. 27, 1984, p. Dff.

Olten, Carol. "Power-assisted tranquility." *San Diego Union*, Feb. 2, 1984.

Ondrechen, Jana. "Two exhibits combine beauty with socio-political statements." *La Jolla Light*, Feb. 2, 1984, p. B9.

Los Angeles County Museum of Art. *Power Places*, Oct. 25–Dec. 30, 1984.

Northlight Gallery, University of Arizona, Tempe. *Power Places*, Apr. 6–May 2.

Tortue Gallery, Santa Monica, California. *Power Places.*

University Art Museum, University of New Mexico, Albuquerque. *Power Places*, Feb. 25–Apr. 1.

Bryant, Edward. "John Pfahl: Power Places." *Artspace* (Albuquerque), Spring 1984, p. 35.

Traugott, Joseph. "Stark Contradictions Give Work Power." *Albuquerque Journal*, Mar. 4, 1984, p. C2.

1985 Media Center Gallery, Webster University, St. Louis, Missouri. *John Pfahl Photography*, Oct. 27–Nov. 23.

1986 Anderson Gallery, School of the Arts, Virginia Commonwealth University, Richmond. *John Pfahl: Photographs from Three Series*, Sept. 9–Oct. 5.

Buscaglia-Castellani Art Gallery of Niagara University, Niagara Falls, New York. *Niagara River and Falls: A Contemporary View*, May 4–Sept. 7.

Huntington, Richard. "Niagara's Beauty, Past and Present." *Buffalo News*, Apr. 27, 1986, pp. E1, E4.

Jones Troyer Gallery, Washington, D.C. *Missile/Glyphs*, Oct. 21–Nov. 29.

Power, Mark. "Photo Art at War with Itself." *The Washington Post*, Nov. 15, 1986, p. C2.

Nina Freudenheim Gallery, Buffalo, New York. *Missile/Glyphs*, Dec. 6, 1986–Jan. 7, 1987.

Chon, Richard. "Photo Juxtapositions Explode With Irony." *Buffalo News*, Dec. 27, 1986, p. B8.

Morgan, Robert. "Binary Fission." *Afterimage* (Rochester, N.Y.), Apr. 1987.

1987 Edwynn Houk Gallery, Chicago. *John Pfahl: Color Work*, Dec. 1–30.

Thall, Larry. "From Color to Computerized, Three Visions of the Landscape." *Chicago Tribune*, Dec. 4, 1987, p. 102ff.

International Museum of Photography at George Eastman House, Rochester, New York. *Power Places*, Sept. 15–Dec. 6.

"Corridor Gallery: Power Places." *International Museum of Photography at George Eastman House Newsletter* (Rochester, N.Y.), Fall 1987, p. 4.

Light Impressions/Spectrum Gallery, Rochester, New York. *Missile/Glyphs*, Nov. 6–Dec. 31.

1988 Buscaglia-Castellani Art Gallery of Niagara University, Niagara Falls, New York. *Power Places*, Apr. 16–Sept. 4.

Fotografie Forum Frankfurt, West Germany. *John Pfahl, Altered Landscapes*.

Photographic Center Northwest, Seattle. *Picture Windows*, Oct. 7–Nov. 9.

Visual Studies Workshop Gallery, Rochester, New York. *Arcadia Revisited: Niagara River and Falls from Lake Erie to Lake Ontario*, Oct. 28, 1988–Jan. 6, 1989. Traveled in 1989–90 to the Rochester Museum and Science Center, New York; Center Gallery, Jamestown Community College, Olean, New York; Florida Gulf Coast Art Center, Belleair, Florida; New Britain Museum of American Art, Connecticut.

Jacobson, Sebby Wilson. "No tricks, only truth." *Times-Union* (Rochester, N.Y.), Aug. 3, 1989, p. 4C.

Reynolds, Judith. "Wasteland, homeland." *City Newspaper* (Rochester, N.Y.), Nov. 3, 1988, p. 13ff.

Simon, Jeff. "Niagara Vistas Echo Earlier Artist." *Buffalo News*, Feb. 2, 1989, p. G9.

Group Exhibitions and Reviews

1971　Central Washington State College, Ellensburg. *New Photographics 71*, May 4–21.

1972　International Museum of Photography at George Eastman House, Rochester, New York. *'60's Continuum*, Feb. 3–May 1.

1976　Centre Culturel Americain, Paris. *Photographie: Rochester, N.Y.*, Apr. 23–June 18. Catalogue, essay by Alan Klotz.

Herbert F. Johnson Museum of Art, Cornell University, Ithaca, New York. *Photo/Synthesis*, Apr. 21–June 6. Catalogue.

1977　Enjay Gallery, Boston. *Color '77*.

Parson, Ann. "Color comes into its own, more than just a mimetic device." *Boston Phoenix*, June 7, 1977, pp. 5, 15.

Everson Museum of Art, Syracuse, New York. *Upstate Color: Michael Bishop, Phil Block, John Pfahl*, Sept. 9–Nov. 13.

1978　Center for Photographic Studies, Louisville, Kentucky. *Colleen and Kathleen Kenyon; John Pfahl*, Feb. 28–Mar. 18.

Cleveland State University.

Colorado Mountain College, Breckenridge. *Recent Works*, July 19–Aug. 7.

Florida School of the Arts, Palatka.

Friends of Photography Gallery, Carmel, California. *Group Show: Color Photographs*.

G. Ray Hawkins Gallery, Los Angeles. *Interrogations into Color*, June 20–July 29.

Johnstone, Mark. "Interrogations into Color." *Artweek* (Oakland, Calif.) July 1, 1978, p. 13.

International Center for Photography, New York.

Niagara County Community College Art Gallery, Sanborn, New York. *Three Photographers from the Freidus Gallery, NYC.*

Niagara Falls Community College, New York.

Silver Image Gallery, Seattle.

Summer Art Festival, Basel, Switzerland.

Summer Art Festival, Bologna, Italy.

University of New Mexico Art Museum, Albuquerque.

University of North Carolina, Charlotte.

Vision Gallery, Boston.

Visual Studies Workshop Gallery, Rochester, New York. *Group Show*, Oct. 13–Nov. 24.

1979   Albright-Knox Art Gallery, Buffalo. *Art for the Vice-President's House from Northeast Museums*, Mar. 6–13.

Albright-Knox Art Gallery, Buffalo. *In Western New York*, Feb. 5–Mar. 4.

   Bannon, Anthony. "WNY Show Runs Gamut of Approaches, Materials." *Buffalo Evening News*, Feb. 6, 1979, p. 10.

   Goldberg, Harold. "Albright-Knox Aesthetics: Modernism and Time-Honored Motifs." *The Spectrum* (Buffalo), Feb. 9, 1979, *Prodigal Sun*, p. 8.

   Willig, Nancy Tobin. "Vigorous Research Evident in W.N.Y. Show at Gallery." *Courier Express* (Buffalo), Feb. 11, 1979, p. F3.

Art Gallery of Cleveland State, organized by NOVA [New Organization for the Visual Arts]. *Photo Electric.*

Art Institute of Chicago. *American Photography in the '70's*, Feb. 3–Mar. 25.

California State University, Fullerton, Art Gallery. *Object, Illusion, Reality*, Sept. 21–Oct. 18. Catalogue, essays by W. Rod Faulds, Darryl Curran, and Eileen Cowin.

Center for Creative Photography, University of Arizona, Tucson. *New Acquisitions: Photographs from the Collection of the Center for Creative Photography*, Mar. 28–May 3.

Colgate University, Hamilton, New York. *John Divola, James Henkel, Bart Parker, John Pfahl*, Oct. 13–Nov. 14.

Inter-Media Art Center, Bayville, New York. *Creative Artists Public Service Program (CAPS) Photo Show*, Aug. 3–Sept. 3.

Huntington, Richard. "CAPS Selections Offer Top Photos." *Buffalo Courier Express*, Sept. 15, 1979, p. 12.

Light Gallery, New York. *Photographs Made with the Polaroid 20 × 24 Camera*, Oct. 1–31.

Milwaukee Art Center. *Colors: A Spectrum of Recent Photography, Part I*, Sept. 6–Oct. 7.

Salon de Photo, Paris.

San Francisco Museum of Modern Art. *Fabricated to be Photographed*, Nov. 16–Dec. 30. Catalogue, essay by Van Deren Coke. Traveled to University Art Museum, University of New Mexico, Albuquerque; Albright-Knox Art Gallery, Buffalo; Great Gallery, Newport Harbor Art Museum, Newport Beach, California.

　Fischer, Hal. "Fabricated to be photographed at the San Francisco Museum of Modern Art." *Afterimage* (Rochester, N.Y.), Mar. 1980, pp. 7–9.

　Huntington, Richard. "Photo Fairytales for Adults on Display at Albright-Knox." *Buffalo Courier Express*, Aug. 10, 1980, pp. E1, E4.

　Murray, Joan. "Fabricated for the Camera." *Artweek* (Oakland, Calif.), Dec. 8, 1979, pp. 11–12.

Muchnic, Suzanne. "Fabricated Photographs on View." *Los Angeles Times*, Oct. 17, 1980.

Santa Barbara Museum of Art, California. *Attitudes: Photography in the 1970's*, May 12–Aug. 5. Catalogue, essay by Fred R. Parker.

Susan Spiritus Gallery, Newport Beach, California. *Henkel, Gordon, Joseph, Pfahl, & others*, Aug. 11–Sept. 22.

Valparaiso University, Indiana. *John Divola, James Henkel, Bart Parker, John Pfahl*, Aug. 28–Sept. 30.

Visual Studies Workshop, Rochester, New York. *John Divola, James Henkel, Bart Parker, John Pfahl*, Oct. 13–Nov. 14.

Williams College, Williamstown, Massachusetts.

1980　Albright College, Reading, Pennsylvania.

Belson-Brown Gallery, Ketchum, Idaho.

Bevier Gallery, Rochester Institute of Technology, New York. *SPAS Faculty Show* [School of Photographic Arts and Sciences at RIT], Oct. 18–Nov. 7.

California Museum of Photography, University of California, Riverside.

Carson-Sapiro Gallery, Denver, Colorado. *New Visions*, July 17–Aug. 30.

Clurman, Irene. "Black and White or Color, Message is Photography." *Rocky Mountain News* (Denver), July 25, 1980, pp. 5, 15C.

Center for Creative Photography, University of Arizona, Tucson. *Reasoned Space*, Apr. 13–May 22. Catalogue, essay by Tim Druckrey and Marnie Gillett.

Columbia Gallery, Missouri.

De Cordova Museum, Lincoln, Massachusetts. *Photography: Recent Directions*, June 1–Aug. 31.

Galerie Rudolf Kicken, Cologne. *Zeitgenossiche Amerikanische Farbphotographie.*

Michael C. Rockefeller Arts Center Gallery, State University of New York at Fredonia. *Two Approaches to Photography: John Pfahl and W. Eugene Smith*, Feb. 2–27.

Philadelphia College of Art. *Polacolor: A Survey of Color and Scale in Recent Polaroid Photography*, Apr. 25–May 24.

Pyramid Gallery, Rochester, New York.

Sewall Art Gallery, Rice University, Houston. *Recent Color Photography: Eight Artists.*

Lee, Karen. "From B & W to Color." *The Rice Thresher* (Houston), Jan. 24, 1980.

Spectrum Photogalerie, Kunstmuseum Hannover, West Germany. *Aspekte Americanischer Farbfotografie*, Dec. 9, 1980–Jan. 12, 1981.

Spencer Museum of Art, University of Kansas, Lawrence.

Hoffman, Donald. "At the galleries: Color photos." *Kansas City Star*, Apr. 20, 1980.

St. Lawrence University, Canton, New York.

University of Iowa, Iowa City. *Four Contemporary American Photographers: Works by Divola, Henkel, Parker and Pfahl*, Oct. 24–Nov. 30.

William Patterson College, Wayne, New Jersey. *Altered Subjects: Photography*, Mar. 10–26.

Yajima Gallery, Montreal, Canada.

Young-Hoffman Gallery, Chicago. *Pfahl, Josephson, Divola, Heinecken*, July–Aug. 9.

Artner, Alan G. "Contemporary photos that touch a conceptional base." *Chicago Tribune*, July 18, 1980.

1981   Arles Festival, France.

Arts Council of Great Britain.

California State University, Fullerton.

Case Western Reserve University, Cleveland.

Chrysler Museum, Norfolk, Virginia. *Contemporary Color Photography*, Jan. 22–Apr. 5.

Denver Art Museum, Colorado. *Selections from the Strauss Photography Collection*, July 10–Nov. 14.

Everson Museum, Syracuse, New York. *The New Color: A Decade of Color Photography*, May 15–July 26. Traveled to International Center for Photography, New York; Columbus Museum of Art, Ohio; Gibbes Art Gallery, Charleston, South Carolina; Art Gallery of Hamilton, Canada.

Davis, Douglas. "A Call to the Colors." *Newsweek* (New York), Nov. 23, 1981, pp. 115–16.

The Handwerker Gallery, Ithaca College, New York. *Light/Color*, Mar. 16–Apr. 12.

International Museum of Photography at George Eastman House, Rochester, New York. *Acquisitions 1973–1980*, June 12–Sept. 13.

James Madison University, Harrisonburg, Virginia.

Laguna Gloria Art Museum, Austin. *Three Photographers: Barboza, Callis, Pfahl*, May 22–July 5.

McAlpin, Pamela. "3 photographers: portrait, still life, landscape." *Daily Texan* (Austin), June 22, 1981.

Mandeville Art Gallery, University of California, San Diego. *Color Photography: New Images.*

Miller, Elise. "New Wave Photography." *San Diego Magazine*, Apr. 1981, p. 97.

Members' Gallery, Albright-Knox Art Gallery, Buffalo. *Area Artists Collection, 1981–82.* May 12–14.

Museum of Art, Rhode Island School of Design, Providence. *Color in Photography*, Apr. 3–May 3.

New York Public Library. *American Photographers and the National Parks.* Traveled to the Minneapolis Institute of Arts.

Phoenix Art Museum.

The Photography Gallery, Toronto, Canada.

The Plaza Gallery, State University of New York, Albany. *The Manipulated Landscape II*, Mar. 13–Apr. 16.

Wright State University, Dayton, Ohio.

1982   Carol Solway Gallery, Cincinnati.

Corcoran Gallery of Art, Washington, D.C. *Color as Form: A History of Color Photography*, Apr. 10–June 6. Traveled to International Museum of Photography at George Eastman House, Rochester, New York.

   Thornton, Gene. "A Color Show Out of Focus." *The New York Times*, Apr. 25, 1982, p. D7.

Friends of Photography, Carmel, California. *Dyed Images: Recent Work in Dye Transfer*, Aug. 27–Sept. 26. Traveled to Art Museum Association of America, San Francisco; Redding Museum of Art, California; Alaska State Museum, Juneau; Visual Arts Center of Alaska, Anchorage; Alaska Association for the Arts, Fairbanks; Museum of Art, Fort Lauderdale, Florida; Charleston Heights Art Center, Las Vegas; El Paso Museum of Art, Texas; University of Puget Sound, Tacoma, Washington; Virginia Polytechnic University, Blacksburg, Virginia; University of Florida, Gainesville; Kaiser Center, Oakland, California; Montgomery Museum of Art, Alabama; Polk County Heritage Gallery, Des Moines.

Georgia State University, Atlanta.

Ithaca College, New York.

New York State Museum, Albany.

Robert Freidus Gallery, New York.

Slusser Gallery, School of Art, University of Michigan, Ann Arbor. *Fugitive Color*, Jan. 9–29. Catalogue, introduction by David Litschel; essay by Diane Kirkpatrick. Traveled in Michigan to Fine Arts Gallery, Central Michigan University, Mount Pleasant; Fine Arts Gallery, Henry Ford Community College, Dearborn; Photography Gallery, Detroit Public Library; Muskegon Museum of Art; Kalamazoo Institute of Arts; Krasl Art Center, St. Joseph; Fine Arts Gallery, Northern Michigan University, Marquette.

State University of New York at Geneseo.

Stockton State College, Pomona, New Jersey. *Photography in Color.*

University of California, San Diego.

University of Colorado, Denver.

University of Texas, Denton.

1983   Albright-Knox Art Gallery, Buffalo, New York. *In Western New York, 1983*. Apr. 8–May 8.

Boise Gallery of Art, Idaho. *Arranged Image Photography*, Oct. 1–Nov. 6. Traveled during 1984–86 to Cheney Cowles Museum, Eastern Washington State Historical Society, Spokane; Yellowstone Art Center, Billings, Montana; Paris Gibson Square, Center for Contemporary Arts, Great Falls, Montana; Hockaday Center for the Arts, Kalispell, Montana; Victoria Museum, Texas.

Centre national d'art et de culture Georges Pompidou, Paris. *Photographes et Paysages, XIX–XXme siècles*.

Nelson-Atkins Museum of Art, Kansas City, Missouri. *New Acquisitions to the Hallmark Photographic Collection 1980–1983*, Apr. 1–May 1.

The Photo Center Gallery, Tisch School of the Arts, New York University. *Photography and the Industrial Image*, Nov. 4–Dec. 1.

   Andre, Linda. "The Rhetoric of Power: Machine Art and Public Relations." *Afterimage* (Rochester, N.Y.), Feb. 1984, pp. 5–7.

Robert Freidus Gallery, New York. *The Television Show: Video Photographs*, Jan. 12–Feb. 5.

Tampa Museum, Florida. *Photography in America: 1910–1983*, Sept. 4–Nov. 6.

1984   Brooklyn Museum, New York. *Color in the Summer*, July 19–Sept. 30.

Caves Sainte Croix, Metz, France. *Construire les paysages de la photographie*, Oct. 5–Nov. 17.

Center for Creative Photography, University of Arizona, Tucson. *Recent Acquisitions*, Dec. 20, 1984–Feb. 13, 1985.

International Museum of Photography at George Eastman House, Rochester, New York. *Rochester, An American Center of Photography: 1827–1984*, Apr. 27–Nov. 20.

Roanoke College, Salem, Virginia. *Divola, Henkel, Parker, Pfahl*, Sept. 1–Oct. 15. Traveled to Everett Community College, Washington.

253, Norfolk, Virginia. *Visions and Vistas*, Dec. 1984–Jan. 11, 1985.

   McGreevy, Linda. "See 253." *Port Folio Magazine* (Norfolk), Dec. 17, 1985.

   Nilsen, Richard. "New Gallery Shows Work of Famed Photographers." *The Virginian-Pilot and The Ledger-Star* (Norfolk), Dec. 8, 1985.

University of Alabama, Tuscaloosa.

University of Northern Iowa, Cedar Falls.

1985   Appalachian Environmental Arts Center, Highlands Biological Station, an Interinstitutional Program of the University of North Carolina administered by Western Carolina University. *Land Escapes: Joys and Sorrows.* Traveled to North Carolina Center for Creative Photography, Durham; The Light Factory, Charlotte; Belk Gallery, Western Carolina University, Cullowhee.

The Barbican Gallery, London. *American Images, 1945–1980.*

    Salway, Kate. "American Images, 1945–1980 at the Barbican, London." *British Journal of Photography* (——————), June 28, 1985, p. 721.

Catskill Center for Photography, Woodstock, New York. *Viewing the Landscape*, Feb. 9–Mar. 19.

    Combs, Tram. "Catskill Center for Photography's Exhibit May Contain Classics." *Sunday Freeman* (Kingston, N.Y.), Feb. 10, 1985, p. 37.

    Isaas, Lei. "New Landscape views at CCFP." *Woodstock Times*, Feb. 14, 1985, pp. 16–17.

DVS Gallery, Taos, New Mexico. *Light Concepts*, May 24–June 23.

International Museum of Photography at George Eastman House, Rochester, New York. *Images of Excellence.* Catalogue, essay by Robert A. Sobieszek.

Metropolitan Museum of Art, New York. *Photographs from the Museum's Collection*, Dec. 4, 1984–Mar. 17, 1985.

Museum of Contemporary Photography, Chicago. *New Color/ New Work: Eighteen Photographic Essays*, Sept. 9–Oct. 12. Catalogue, essay by Sally Eauclaire.

Pratt Manhattan Center Gallery, New York. *Illuminating Color: Four Approaches in Contemporary Painting and Photography*, Sept. 9–Oct. 5. Traveled to Pratt Institute Gallery, Brooklyn, New York.

    Glueck, Grace. "Illuminating Color." *The New York Times*, Sept. 20, 1985.

San Francisco Museum of Modern Art. *Extending the Perimeters of Twentieth-Century Photography*, Aug. 2–Oct. 6.

University Gallery, University of Massachusetts at Amherst. *Ten*, Sept. 14–Oct. 25. Catalogue, introduction by Helaine Posner.

Western Carolina University, Cullowhee, North Carolina. *Altered Landscapes*, Jan. 14–Feb. 1.

1986   Afterimage Photo Gallery, Dallas. *The Moon Show*, Sept. 13–Oct. 25.

    Collmer, Kathryn. "Etcetera: Shooting the Moon." *Southwest Art* (Houston), Feb. 1987, pp. 80–81.

    Aldrich Museum of Contemporary Art, Ridgefield, Connecticut. *Views and Visions: Recent American Landscape Photography.*

    Atrium Gallery, University of Connecticut, Storrs. *Masterworks of Contemporary Photography*, Sept. 22–Oct. 3.

    Bruno Facchetti Gallery, New York. *Acceptable Entertainment.*

    International Center of Photography, New York. *Views and Visions: Recent American Landscape Photography.*

    Museum of Fine Arts, Museum of New Mexico, Santa Fe. *Poetics of Space*, Dec. 19, 1986–Mar. 22, 1987.

    Laurent, Amy. "Capturing the Poetics of Space." *Artweek* (Oakland, Calif.), Jan. 17, 1987.

    Ludlow, Cynthia. "Explorations of Space." *Santa Fe Reporter*, Dec. 22, 1986, pp. 22, 24.

    Meriwether, Cissie, and Harrison Sudborough. "Oh unusual, for spacious art." *New Mexican* (Santa Fe), Dec. 26, 1986.

    Plett, Nicole. "Space is Key to New Tack in Art." *Albuquerque Journal*, Feb. 1, 1987, pp. E1, E10.

    San Francisco Museum of Modern Art. *Photography: A Facet of Modernism*, Dec. 5, 1986–Mar. 15, 1987. Catalogue, essay by Van Deren Coke with Diana C. du Pont.

    Visual Studies Workshop, Rochester, New York. *Photography: A Regional Survey*, Oct. 18–Dec. 5.

1987   Friends of Photography Gallery, Carmel, California. *Twentieth Anniversary Exhibition*, Aug. 17–Sept. 27.

    John Michael Kohler Arts Center, Sheboygan, Wisconsin. *Visual Paradox: Truth and Fiction in the Photographic Image*, Dec. 6, 1987–Feb. 14, 1988.

    Los Angeles County Museum of Art. *Photography and Art: Interactions Since 1945*, June 4–Aug. 30. Catalogue, essay by Andy Grundberg and Kathleen McCarthy Gauss. Traveled to Museum of Art, Fort Lauderdale, Florida; Queens Museum, Flushing, New York; Des Moines Art Center.

    Min Gallery, Tokyo.

    Minneapolis Institute of Arts. *Photographs Beget Photographs*, Jan. 24–Mar. 29. Catalogue, essay by Christian A. Peterson. Traveled to Grand Rapids Art Museum, Michigan; Madison Art Center, Wisconsin; de Saisset Museum, Santa Clara University,

California; Neuberger Museum, State University of New York at Purchase; University Art Museum, California State University, Long Beach; Art Gallery of Hamilton, Canada; Sioux City Art Center, Iowa; Laguna Gloria Art Museum, Austin.

Museum Ludwig, Cologne. *Von Landschaftsbild zur Spurensicherung.*

1988   Art Institute of Chicago. *Recent Acquisitions from the Permanent Collection,* Nov. 22, 1988–Jan. 22, 1989.

Blue Sky, Oregon Center for the Photographic Arts, Portland. *New Photographics Invitational,* Dec. 1–31.

The Handwerker Gallery, Ithaca College, New York. *Vanishing Point.*

Houston Foto Festival. *Windows,* Feb.–Apr.

Queens Museum, Flushing, New York. *Photography and Art: Interactions Since 1945,* Feb. 17–Apr. 3.

Sarah Spurgeon Gallery, Central Washington University, Ellensburg. *New Photographics Invitational,* Nov.

Glowen, Ron, "Expanding Photographic Concepts." *Artweek* (Oakland, Calif.), Nov. 12, 1988, pp. 11, 12.

"Nationally acclaimed artists visit for show, seminars." *Daily Record* (Ellensburg, Wash.), Oct. 24, 1988.

Stillman, Lillian. "Art on film: Reviewer brings 'New Photographics' invitational show into focus." *Daily Record* (Ellensburg, Wash.), Nov. 4, 1988, p. 2.

Schwanenburg Fotogalerie, Kleve, West Germany. *Veranderten Landschaften,* Apr. 17–May 26.

Tower Fine Arts Gallery, State University of New York at Brockport. *New Approaches to Landscape Art.*

Netsky, Ron. "Fresh Looks, Familiar Views." *Democrat and Chronicle* (Rochester, N.Y.), Mar. 10, 1988, p. 3D.

1989   Center for Creative Photography, University of Arizona, Tucson. *Decade by Decade: Twentieth-Century American Photography from the Collection of the Center for Creative Photography,* Feb. 10–June 9. Traveled to Phoenix Art Museum.

Emma Woods Gallery, Santa Barbara Museum of Art, California. *Attitudes Revisited,* July 1–Sept. 10.

International Museum of Photography at George Eastman House, Rochester, New York. *New Acquisitions/New Work/New Directions,* May 12–Sept. 10.

National Gallery of Art, Washington, D.C. *On the Art of Fixing a Shadow: One Hundred and Fifty Years of Photography,* May 7–July 30. Traveled to the Art Institute of Chicago and Los Angeles County Museum of Art.

Santa Barbara Contemporary Art Forum, California. *Beaches: An Exhibition of Work by 20 Photographers*, Aug. 19–Sept. 16.

Visual Studies Workshop Gallery, Rochester, New York. *Visual Studies Workshop Gallery Artists*, Mar. 16–July 28.

1990   The Museum of Fine Arts, Houston. *Money Matters: A Critical Look at Bank Architecture*, Feb. 4–Apr. 5. Traveled to the National Building Museum, Washington, D.C.; Canadian Centre for Architecture, Montreal; Chicago Historical Society; Vancouver Museum, British Columbia; National Gallery, Ottawa; and Royal Ontario Museum, Toronto.

A DISTANCED LAND
The Photographs of John Pfahl

Edited by Mary Cochrane (Albright-Knox Art Gallery) and
Dana Asbury (University of New Mexico Press)
Designed by Milenda Nan Ok Lee
Typography in Trump Mediaeval
by the University of New Mexico Printing Services

Printed by Dai Nippon Printing Co., Ltd.
Printed in Japan

Photograph Credits
Color
All color plates are by John Pfahl.
Black and White
Gianfranco Gorgoni, New York: p. 8
K.C. Kratt, Buffalo: p. 178
National Archives, Washington, D.C.: p. 21
Courtesy of the artist: pp. 5, 171

Jacket and cover illustrations:
front, *Bethlehem #16*, 1988, from *Smoke*, 1988–;
back, *Moonrise over Pie Pan*, 1977, from *Altered Landscapes*, 1974–78; 1980.